KILL THE INDIAN, SAVE THE CHILD:
THE RESIDENTIAL SCHOOL TRAGEDY OF AGONI BLUE CLOUD

Vern Seefeldt

NEWMAN SPRINGS PUBLISHING
320 Broad Street
Red Bank, NJ 07701

First originally published by Newman Springs Publishing 2024

ISBN 979-8-89308-708-6 (Paperback)
ISBN 979-8-89308-709-3 (Digital)

Printed in the United States of America

To Nancy, whose love, devotion, and courage
provided the foundation for our fifty-five wonderful years;
to daughter Lynne and son-in-law Jesse;
to son John and daughter-in-law Karen;
to grandchildren Kayla and Ross
for your ceaseless affection, companionship, and care.
We are eternally grateful.

Contents

List of illustrations by Ricardo Capraro

Disclaimer

The dates, events, and locations in this book are written to portray the realistic environment during the early twentieth century, at a time when the conscription of Indigenous children was at its summit in Canada and the United States. The names of all individuals and places are pseudonyms to protect the identity of places and persons, living or dead, and the environment in which they lived. The word *Indian* is used in the narrative because the term was commonly written by governmental officials and in reports of the media in the early twentieth and twenty-first centuries, with reference to Native people who inhabited northern British Columbia. The author is aware that the terms *Native Americans, Indigenous People, First Nations*, and specific tribal names such as Tagish, Inland Tlingit, and Kaska are currently preferred, but for purposes of authenticity, the term *Indian* is used in the narrative.

Acknowledgments

Children, wherever they live, have been an accessible, ever-present laboratory for observation and study. Their innocence, honesty, and quest for learning, combined with an incessant willingness to repeat challenges in the face of failure, are admirable characteristics that deserve preservation for a lifetime. Innate attempts to learn physical, intellectual, and social skills are universal traits, unless they are suppressed by exposure to inappropriate increments or by socially repressed ways of behavior. My opportunity to observe children in eight countries reinforced the knowledge that these admirable characteristics are present regardless of race, color, creed, or gender.

Changes in present societies have reduced the necessity of skills required for subsistence, shelter, and security; currently replaced by adaptations to electronic modes for academic achievement, ambulation, and communication. The facility with which children have adjusted to new ways of formal education is a testament to their versatility. Despite greater opportunities for motoric skills, this area of development appears to receive reduced attention, except for those who demonstrate unusual prowess. Environments controlled by adults must continue to allocate appropriate time for the comprehension and acquisition of skills that are essential for human well-being.

A tribute to children everywhere would be incomplete if it did not include a request to adults who are responsible for their care and education. Children's quest for independence continues until adulthood, but the journey requires supervision and guidance. The lines between independence and control are delicate, frequently interchangeable during the growing process, and breached when constraint is not present. Opportunities to master developmental skills build the foundation for complex skills. Sedentary living deprives children of this repertoire. Freedom of movement and exploration provide the basic requirements for a lifetime of healthful activity. Adults remain custodians of these opportunities.

Prologue

The story that follows is designated as *historical fiction*, but it has a personal association with the author, whose father became acquainted with a group of conscripted native children who were on their way to enrollment in one of the provincial residential schools. The children had just arrived in Hazelton, British Columbia, via cedar dugout canoes from their home on the upper Skeena River. The time was August 1925, when my father and his partner traveled as homesteaders into the British Columbian wilderness in search of furs, fish, and game. Their destination was the Skeena Valley, north of the Gitxsan First Nation Tribe's permanent encampment.

Hazelton, British Columbia, was the homesteaders' official point of departure when they were surrounded by a group of approximately twenty-five native children. Barney and Louie had just mounted their horses, each leading two pack animals, ready to begin their four-day journey to their assigned homesteads. Children repeatedly called "Can-dee, can-dee," asking the men for a delicacy to which they had most likely been introduced by adults who had visited the military commissary. Taken by surprise, my father and his partner dismounted, and through a combination of verbal and sign language, told the children they would go to the commissary and return.

They were told by provincial Agent Blackstone that the children were being taken to a residential school as part of the Canadian government's way of reeducating them to a civilized way of life. My father and his partner bought packaged cookies, distributed them to the waiting children, and continued their journey. My father retained this upsetting occurrence his entire life, reflecting on how any civilized organization could justify taking five- to six-year-old children from their biological parents to change their lifestyle. Even more troublesome were two provisions of the deployment: Government Agent Blackstone informed them the children would be educated by Christian missionaries, whose accepted precept was *kill the Indian, save the child*; the governmental order to send the children to residential schools was considered an acceptable way of *civilizing them* in the minds of the Canadian citizens whom they met in Prince Rupert and at the military depot.

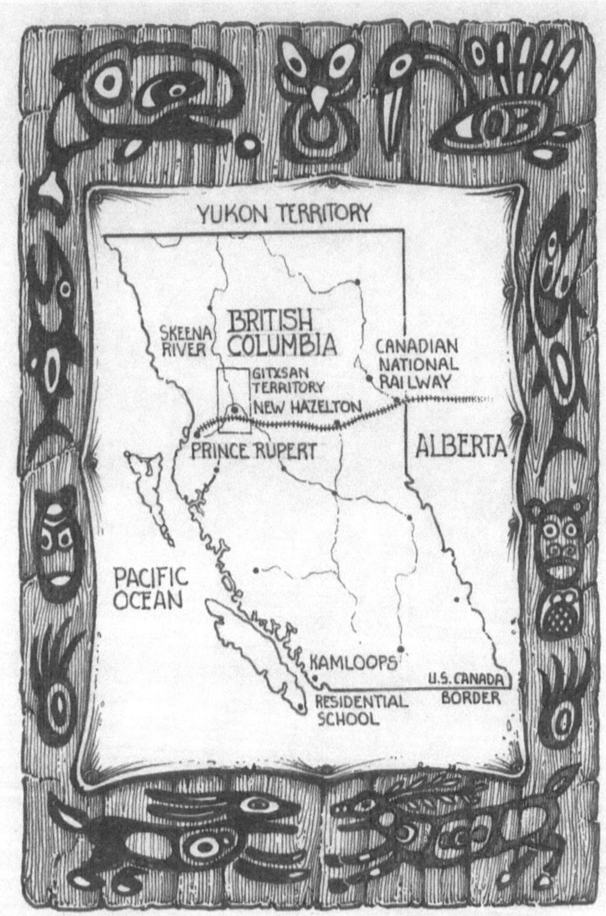

Fig. 1 Territorial map of the Gitxsan Nation

Daily Life of the Eagle Clan, Gitxsan Tribe

"Wait," called Agent Blackstone, his extended arm containing a telegram as he ran to the landing where Chief Grey Eagle was about to launch his canoe for the Eagle Clan's encampment.

His excitement led to shouting the contents of the telegram before he reached the landing. "This is a directive from the White Father in Ottawa, ordering you to send your children to English schools this fall, so they can learn White man's ways."

"Children no go," emphatically stated Grey Eagle. "No need English school."

Grey Eagle's instinctive reply frustrated Agent Blackstone. "I told you some time ago, the Canadian government wants all children to be healthy and pay their own way as Canadian citizens. The Gitxsan Nation has not sent its children to the schools. If you do not send them, the military will come for them."

"No go," declared Grey Eagle. "Soldiers come, Eagle Clan, with rifles, behind every tree."

Grey Eagle's statement about his clan's resistance to the children's removal alarmed Agent Blackstone. His responsibility was to prevent confrontations between the First Nations people and the white settlers who were coming to British Columbia in response to Canada's new Homestead Act. The contentious situation ended when Grey Eagle, in anger, launched his canoe and paddled upstream to his encampment.

Arrival at the Eagle Clan's permanent residence by their Chief was usually the cause for excitement. Grim-faced Chief Grey Eagle's posture told the children, "Do not approach me."[1]

Grey Eagle told his clan that visiting the Depot had been disappointing. He walked to the wilp and instructed the members of his council, which included all males aged sixteen and older, to meet immediately. Council members were seated around the firepit when Grey Eagle presented the most serious dilemma his clan had faced recently. Eagle Clan members had prepared for war numerous times, but quarrels with the Canadian government were a new kind of encounter.

"White men in Ottawa say we send children to English school," announced Chief Grey Eagle, whose manner had alerted his council that the reason for the meeting was troublesome. "How we stop Ottawa's orders?" he asked. "Have do so years. Order from Ottawa tells must act now to keep children here."

"Children not go to their school," stated Waban, leader of the Territorial Patrol, who had successfully repulsed the Dene challenge three years ago. His accuracy with the clan's newly acquired weapons—thirty-thirty carbine rifles—had changed their method of warfare and emboldened their reaction to foreign challenges. Bullets had four times the range of their former weapons: arrows, spears, and knives. His bold statement was received with agreement by the council, who nodded their approval.

"Fighting increases government's action," protested Chief Grey Eagle, who had survived numerous scrimmages with local governments over treaty rights.

"Agree," said Blue Cloud, a new member of the Eagle Clan, an exceptional acquisition because of his marriage to Metonka, the daughter of Grey Eagle. "Should move wilp far upriver, our land. They fight, we in better place help ourselves."

---

[1]   In 1867, Canada enacted the *British North American Act*, which required the Canadian government to provide education for Indigenous children. This Act was passed without the government having any knowledge of the numbers involved, nor the budgetary requirements to support the Act.

After a long discussion, Grey Eagle, realizing that his suggestion to avoid confrontation with the government was not in concert with the opinions held by most of the council members, called for a vote to empower a new leader for the clan, an act tantamount to resignation. His request resulted in the election of Waban as Chief and Blue Cloud as head of the Territorial Patrol.

Newly elected Chief Waban, aware of the urgency apparent in the government's directive, ordered the Territorial Patrol to seek a new encampment, as suggested by Blue Cloud. Suitable sites for encampments on the banks of the Skeena River were plentiful, as reported by the patrol. Eagle Clan members accepted the decision to move without complaints when they understood its motive. Children had become accustomed to the frequent boat and canoe traffic at their present site, so the requirement to move was not pleasing to them. Adults remembered their former move from the Pacific Ocean to the Skeena River; thus, they reluctantly accepted the reason for deployment and willingly participated in the move to their new location.

Moving the Eagle Clan's encampment eighty miles upriver required energy and cooperation. Early May was an excellent season for such a move, allowing sufficient time to determine ideal sites for gathering and hunting, which were accessible and abundant in their new location—hitherto, both having been free of human disturbances.

Exploration became a necessary activity for adults and children. Meadows, hills, rocks, rivers, and streams offered opportunities for gathering and hunting, now available in immeasurable numbers. Isolation, initially the common sentiment of children, was soon overridden by daily preparations for subsistence and, ultimately, survival. Family dwellings and a wilp required construction, storage space for dried fruits and berries required dugouts in hillsides, and drying racks for jerky of fish and venison awaited construction.

The rigors of settlement in the new encampment were soon erased by physical and emotional relief. Yet, in the minds of Chief Waban and patrol leader Blue Cloud, there existed a premonition that the move was a temporary solution. The relentless search for land by the pioneers and the zeal of Christian religious organizations posed problems that had previously been insurmountable. Both men knew of the troublesome, historic attempts by Indigenous people to seek justice and freedom. Would their move upstream provide the solace and peace they sought, or was this the calm before another impending storm?

Chief Waban and former Chief Grey Eagle were young men when their village was forced to move from the banks of the Pacific Ocean, in a two-hundred-mile journey inland, to the military post of Hazelton. Escaping the aggressive encroachment of white settlers on their ancestral fishing grounds was necessary for survival. The current situation presented similar options. Both men agreed it was time to call on historian Story Teller Haida for consultation.

Education, religion, and counsel were entwined characteristics of daily life in the clan. Purveying these essential elements was entrusted to older men who had survived numerous tribulations associated with Indigenous life in a harsh environment. They made arrangements to call ex-Chief Haida, a member of the neighboring Shuswap Tribe, to inform clan members of their history and, more importantly, projection for the future of the Gitxsan Nation.

Members of the Eagle Clan were seated around the firepit when Story Teller Haida began a historic lesson that would take two evenings in its telling. He stood, sat, sang, danced, and shouted to emphasize specific parts of his lesson. Children, usually asleep with boredom in similar situations, watched and listened with amazement as they learned about their ancestors.

Storyteller Haida began his lesson by stating, "Tonight I tell you about life long ago. Many things I tell you are like today. Gitxsan means 'people of the river mist' because water from Skeena and Babine mountains comes from snow and ice. Come to warm air, bring mist." His recollection of the clan's history intrigued young and older members. He stated that the Gitxsan Tribes migrated to the headwaters of the Skeena River, British Columbia, Canada, in 1870, to escape the oppressive rules of the recently federalized Canadian government. Passage of the 1867 British North American Act required the Canadian government to provide education for all Indigenous children. This Act was viewed by the Gitxsan nation as an infringement of their historical, unwritten code of independence. Governmental officials had decreed the nomadic ways of its First Nations people were not sufficiently stable nor economically adequate to support their children. This belief existed despite decades of evidence that their lifestyle was a sustainable and enduring way of life for numerous First Nations Tribes, capable of supporting families despite the rigors of Canada's frequently harsh winter environment.

"Our people live many years in south place of Skeena River, named Skeena County, land of thirty-three thousand-kilometer land and water, like Hazleton, Babine, Kispiox, Bulkley, and Skeena Rivers. We fight keep land. Believe take care of ourselves. Can care for lands, rule our people."

Storyteller Haida continued by telling the clan of their present history. "Our people always be ruled by squaws, mean our line based on females. Child born in one of four clans (Frog, Eagle, Wolf, or Fireweed). People not marry in own clan. Family house called wilp, all clan stay winter moons. Wilps needed because each wilp rule land and fishing place. Fishing place go to males born to mother in each wilp. All family live in small home, of cedar posts, with roof and sides covered with bark, caribou hides, and grass. We good at things learned long ago, like storytelling, weaving, carvings bone, make totem poles. Language sound like Tsimshian, say we like our neighbors on Pacific coast, place we come moons ago.

"We live on shores and forests off Pacific Ocean, get there walking over land bridge (now the Bering Straits), fifteen thousand winter moons before Ice come. Great-great-grandfathers' first touch with no ice land along Pacific Coast, life there made easy catch fish and shellfish in warm water. Big boats, many moon years ago, drive us to land along south Skeena River till it go west, at place now Hazelton. We stay one tribe, chief be ruling head. Clans be friendly with other clans, by rule marriage in clan not possible, so always peace with other clans."

Storyteller stopped and said, "This all for tonight. Tomorrow, I tell how we live like today." The next evening, his audience waited in anticipation to learn why they lived in the same large house, why they all ate from the same pot of stew, how they learned to catch fish, how they learned to harness dogs to sleds, why the women did all the work in the encampment, and only men hunted and fished.

"Lives ruled by sex and age," said Haida. "Care young children early work of mother, first two years child's life close to her, carry in arms or on cradleboard. Two years, child go free play any place any area camp. Child then care of all clan. Old people where child play now helpers. Children not punished by hands. Taking away good things, make shame, make stay away from friends best ways to punish. Children know by watch old people. Scold, shout, and angry words for changes come from bad parents.

"Free live always there in child's day, like eat, sleep, and play. Child follow parents' way of live. Food always there in the wilp. Child rest or sleep in own house, or take caribou blanket to wilp for sleep with friend so be happy while sleep.

"We live either eat much or not enough. Work hard last full moons of summer. Know our good feel in winter be on what we find keep in last six moons. Deep snow water freeze, make end to hunt and find food. Chief every day look at food storage space, in cave dig in side of hill, tell if roots, berries, salmon, deer and elk jerky, honey, and maple candy plenty for food in dark winter days when sun not higher than treetops.

"Deep snows stop moving outside, but help cover roofs and sides of homes and wilp. Fireplace in center wilp keep warm. Squaws care of firewood, kept near wilp. Ground floor sweep every day with branch of Norway spruce tree. Families stay same space in wilp— warm by how close to fireplace. Caribou hides, hair cut short for rugs. Soft tanned deer hides for blankets. Child sleep with parents, under same cover, cold weather uses tanned caribou hides wrap around, like sleep bag.

"Child learn food come outside. We go foot or canoe, where food find. Spring bring roots of water plants, smelt and suckers in river, on land wild strawberries, blueberries, blackberries, cherries, apples, and pears, eat when can find. Food not eat, dry for take to cave.

"Hunt and fish do by men. Many animals live in Skeena Valley. Bighorn sheep in Skeena and Babine mountains. Deer, moose, caribou, and elk in big woods of beech, oak, and cedar tree. Big animals moose and caribou shot, bring to camp by dogs, pull sleds made moose hides when snow not there for sled runners.

"Fish in Skeena River catch by nets of caribou sinews. Spring time when small streams be full of golden and Dolly Varden trout, come to shallow water for spawning. Streams come to river have northern pike, speared for tender meat and roe, in spawning time. Salmon best food, protein for people and dogs, swim many side streams of Skeena River to spawn.

"Eat in summer and fall come what food can find, meat, fish, or berries. Food not eat dried and keep till come home. Food then in hillside caves, ready for cold days.

"People not hunt and find food busy with arts of tribe. Women cut, dry, weave rugs, clothes, blankets from animal skins and soft, inner bark of cedar tree. Girls work with squaw, learn how find and store food and wood, get meat of large animals, salmon for jerky. Meals cook over open fire. Squaw fix outsides of home, make wilp clean, ready for all clan. Fish or meat bring to camp for cook done by squaw and girls. Heavy work, long ago for men, now do by women, early years, fight often take men of village, then squaw learn do work like men.

"Children never told do work or how to live. Ways and lives of old people show to do. Keep from friends is most hard kind of punishment for young and old, many times lead to alone and starve; show ways can live, but not to do by us."

When Storyteller Haida finished his lesson, Chief Waban asked, "You tell us of live long ago. Same problems today. What do now?"

Storyteller Haida pointed his index finger at the roof of the wilp, in a northern direction. He held up his left hand to indicate silence, sat cross-legged near the firepit, and began to move his soundless lips. The people of the clan knew by his posture that he was praying to the North Star, the ever-present, nighttime beacon of direction for First Native Tribes. He arose and addressed the clan leaders and their patrol.

"Yes, some same, but some change. Have rifles, not run like before. Now live where soldiers not like fight. Two big changes."

"How we fight government that take our children?" asked Blue Cloud.

"Government give food and tools. Not good. Find food for two years, so eat when government not send food. Get rifles and shells, teach boys and men to shoot. Get all wilps ready to fight. Ottawa change school law when you show fight. Children go schools near home. Ottawa not want to fight. Far-off schools bad for children. Show angry about law. Show fight to change law."

Storyteller Haida's forecast and suggested solutions met the approval of Blue Cloud and Chief Waban. Moving to their new location would delay the impending battle and give the clan time to prepare. They would develop the new encampment and, for the present, resume their hunting and gathering way of life, hoping that Ottawa's mandate would not follow them. Peace and reduced anxiety restored the happy lifestyle of the Eagle Clan as they prepared for the coming winter in their usual manner.

Fig. 2 Agoni, age one year, and Metonka, age twenty-six years

Introduction of Characters

Kwantum (meaning "big boy-big man") was the son of Louie Harris, an American hunter and trapper originally from the state of Kansas, USA, and Metonka, who met Harris while escaping from an abusive relationship with her then-husband, Chief Hucum. Metonka and Harris cohabited in Harris's cabin until Metonka was forcibly returned to her home by the Eagle Clan's Territorial Patrol, led by Chief Hucum, who was killed during the rescue encounter. Kwantum was the resultant son of the relationship between Metonka and Harris.

Kwantum, according to his mother, had the long arms and legs of his father, who was six feet four inches tall. He demonstrated his athletic ability at an early age, impatient to get out of the cradleboard at the age of four months, which was the customary daytime home of children until they were two years old. Kwantum's ever-ready smile endeared him to everyone he met. His engaging personality and advanced motor skills allowed him to play with boys two or three years older than he. Precocious characteristics such as these also persuaded his adopted father, Blue Cloud, to take him on hunting and fishing trips at twelve years of age—two years before the customary marker of maturity for boys in the clan.

Metonka was the daughter of Grey Eagle, the former chief of the Eagle Clan, whose present encampment was on the banks of the Skeena River, eighty miles north of the train depot in Hazelton, British Columbia. Ex-Chief Grey Eagle, in failing health due to aging, had recently been replaced by Chief Hucum. Metonka, age fifteen, a beautiful maiden, was commanded by Chief Hucum to come to his wilp, where she became his fourth wife. This union (marriage) was forbidden because it involved members of the same clan. Chief

Hucum declared that it was not a marriage, despite evidence to the contrary. The first year of their arranged marriage was as Metonka expected, in her role as a dutiful woman in the Eagle Clan. A year thereafter, Chief Hucum's usually affectionate nature changed, which led to physical abuse during his now frequent bouts with alcohol. The abuse became intolerable, causing Metonka to pack her meager belongings and, traveling on snowshoes, head up the frozen Skeena River, intending to seek relief at Hazelton. During this attempted escape, she met Louie Harris. Frightened, hungry, and exhausted, she accepted Harris's invitation to stay in his cabin until she felt able to continue her travels. Harris's invitation continued for four months until it was interrupted by the Territorial Patrol. Metonka, now pregnant, was forced to accompany the patrol back to her encampment. Mysteriously, Harris's disappearance was never solved—Harris was never seen or heard from again.

Blue Cloud had been a member of the Wolf Clan, a neighboring clan that lived to the east of the territory claimed by the Eagle Clan. Blue Cloud met Metonka at the annually held potlatches, which were traditional social events between clans. During the customary dance, women could not enter the dance area unless invited by men. Frequent invitations by Blue Cloud to Metonka led to romance, which led to marriage and Blue Cloud's membership in the Eagle Clan. Blue Cloud's physical strength and pleasant personality soon elevated him to a position of leadership, with implications for chiefdom. The change in clan leadership led to his position as leader of the Territorial Patrol.

Agoni (pronounced "Ah-gon-ee," meaning "little butterfly") was the second child of Metonka and the first child of Blue Cloud. Agoni was born when Kwantum was nine years old. She was linear like her mother, with black hair two inches long at birth. Her beautiful, black hair, thin in diameter, would become a trademark, flowing in the wind as she ran at play. Little sister was the highlight of Kwantum's life. Agoni idolized Kwantum, and the feeling was mutual. Whenever she saw Kwantum, her face broke into a smile reserved for the few people among the many with whom she had contact.

Agoni's resistance to being placed in the cradleboard began at two months of age. Her protests involved total body squirming, kicking her legs, waving her arms, and whining until her mother relented by placing her on a deerskin blanket, where she showed her pleasure by constant movement. Freedom from the cradleboard was made possible by the devoted attention of Kwantum, who was her daily attendant during her waking hours. Freedom of movement hastened her physical and social skills, allowing her to explore the encampment as soon as she could walk—an opportunity denied to other children until they were two years old. Agoni showed an unusual curiosity for the activities of adults, frequently questioning how and why certain actions and events were part of clan life. She spoke at an early age, most likely stimulated by her mobility and need for social interaction.

Griffin was a dog of mixed genealogy, whose father was a malamute sled dog and whose mother was a gray wolf (*Canis lupus*). Griffin was found as an abandoned puppy by Grey Eagle on one of his autumn hunting trips. Griffin was abandoned because the Bulkley Wolf Pack, as with any of the resident packs, did not permit mixed genealogy within its members. Griffin's mother paid dearly for her indiscretion, relegated to the end of the breeding line within the pack, which meant that she would never be pregnant again. She was not allowed to eat from carcasses until all had eaten, nor could she join the pack on its daily hunts. Instead, she was given the task of puppy care while the other members enjoyed the challenging hunt. Pack membership required abandoning her pups—thus, Griffin's status when he was found by Grey Eagle.

Grey Eagle gave Griffin to Kwantum, who accepted his new friend with the affection reserved for best friends. Boy and dog became inseparable companions—one depending on the other for food, love, and companionship, and the other in reciprocation provided assurance and protection during the boyhood days of adventure in a frequently dangerous environment. As the companion of Grey Eagle's grandson, Griffin was granted special privileges.

Although Griffin eventually became the lead dog on the sled team, he was not tied up as were the other members of the team. He was allowed to roam freely, in the company of Kwantum, thereby assuring adults of the clan that both were safely engaged in some activity.

Storyteller Haida was a historian, educator, prophet, and medicine man. Storytellers were the most revered persons in tribal lore. Usually reserved for elderly, experienced men, the title was accorded by reputation to those renowned for memory and teaching ability. Storytelling was an intertribal, itinerant position, accomplished by requests from the chief of a tribe or clan. Storytelling was an annual event, held in open-air classrooms during seasonable weather, and around the wilp firepit in winter.

Chief Hucum assumed his leadership position because of his skills as a warrior. As a young man, he stepped forward in the battle of Babine, in which he led the Eagle Clan's resistance to the invading Babine tribe, thereby retaining the northernmost border of the Gitxsan territory. His addiction to alcohol eroded his clan's trust, which led to Metonka's escape and his death during her attempted recovery by her clan.

Chief Waban, successor of Chief Hucum, was nominated because Blue Cloud, the heir apparent, was a recent member of the Eagle Clan. Limited by advanced age, Chief Waban was chosen because of reminiscence rather than ability. Early in Grey Eagle's chiefdom, he led the Territorial Patrol in its frequent scrimmages against the homesteaders, who believed that the territory historically held by the Gitxsan Tribe was now available to anyone who filed a claim. Older clan members remembered the leadership provided by Chief Waban as a defender of their present encampment. When the opportunity arose, they awarded him with the chiefdom.

Provincial Agent Jim Blackstone was chosen for his post because of his mixed heritage and his familiarity with negotiations between Indigenous tribes and the Canadian government. His mother was of the Tsimshian Tribe, who resided on the Pacific Coast. His father was a French-Canadian citizen employed by the Hudson Bay Fur Company. His assigned task of facilitating negotiations between local natives and the Canadian government often left him in a compromised position. He was keenly aware of the Gitxsan's vigorous fight for self-determination. He also realized that governmental laws and regulations were systematically stripping away these rights.

Factor Leon McKensey was an aspirational member of the Montreal Commission on Indian Affairs. His rapid rise in the administrative hierarchy, leading to an appointment at the prestigious Ottawa Provincial Commission, was not lost on the perception of current Commissioner McNeil. McKensey's ability to continue his resume building was halted when McNeil assigned McKensey to the post as Factor of Indian Affairs in Prince Rupert, British Columbia— "the end of the world" as Mrs. McKensey referred to the assignment. Intent on maintaining his unblemished reputation as a fastidious administrator, McKensey followed the letter of the law as issued by the Canadian government. He knew his return to Ottawa depended on maintaining peaceful relations with First Nations Tribes—a task made more difficult by the independence of Gitxsan members, who resided in the most popular area of provincial expansion, exclusive of the Pacific Coast.

Kamloops Regional Director of Indian Affairs Samuel McLeod was responsible for the administration of Crown land, including the rapidly growing city of Kamloops. Recently, he had acquired a new assignment. The growth of the residential school added an additional administrative burden—one which he wished he had been able to avoid or assign to someone in his administration. Budget responsibilities in his jurisdiction had, in the last seven years, increased by five hundred students, a support staff of 250 adults, and the cost of buildings, food, and labor to support the government's new venture of educating Indigenous children. The budget now included funds from the Catholic Church, which were always in arrears for its expenditures of food and clothing to support the growing number of occupants at the residential school. His view about the best way to educate Indigenous children conflicted with the strongly held opinion of School Superintendent Crosswhite.

School Superintendent Ms. Crosswhite was assigned to the Kamloops Residential School because of her reputation as a no-nonsense teacher and administrator in Ottawa's ghetto area schools. Her persuasion as a staunch religious parishioner solidified her application as a candidate for the influential but challenging position of Kamloops Residential School's educational leader. She immediately sought to establish her realm of command by publishing a memorandum outlining the duties of assistant administrators, teachers, maintenance personnel, and custodians. Control was incomplete because Director McLeod, at the top of the chain of command, did not believe in the forced removal of children for religious education. Differences regarding the education of children became greater with the passage of time. Director McLeod believed day schools were a more effective way to assimilate native children, in direct opposition to the complete-eradication model now in effect at Kamloops Residential School.

Teacher June Ames, a first-year teacher from Vancouver, British Columbia, was imbued with the chance to assist needy students. An offer from the Kamloops Residential School seemed the ideal place to practice her newly acquired wisdom. June possessed a year of Native Languages and Culture as part of her baccalaureate degree from the University of Vancouver. She was aware of the controversy surrounding residential schools. Nothing in her education had prepared her for the challenges she was about to face at Kamloops. Prescribed procedures of teaching, as mandated by Superintendent Crosswhite, were in direct conflict with the recommended methods she had perfected as an intern in Vancouver's public schools.

Head Soccer Coach Jake Jones was a former star of the Vancouver soccer team. He and assistant coach Nester were Kamloops dock administrators, who acquired their volunteer positions by convincing Director McLeod that boys at Kamloops Residential School should join the regional soccer league. His wish was granted on the condition that he assume the position of head coach. He then recruited his coworker, Frank Nester, to become his assistant. Soccer was an instant success with the Gitxsan boys because it resembled a run, kick, and throw game they played on the sandy beaches of the Pacific Ocean and the plains of the Skeena River.

Fig. 3 Wilp (longhouse: Eagle Clan's winter home)

Kwantum, Agoni, and Griffin:
An Ideal Life in the Eagle Clan

Autumn was the most beautiful time of year in the village of the Eagle Clan. Enemies to the far north had not recovered from their last attempt to occupy the territory claimed by the present occupants. Spring arrived early in the valley, bringing with it abundant patches of blueberries, currants, huckleberries, and gooseberries. Hickory and oak trees were laden with mast. Reports from Prince Rupert suggested the salmon run would be early. Deer, elk, and woodland caribou grazed in the meadows, unaware their safety was attributable to the warm weather, which caused early jerky to become moldy.

Men were cutting the fallen oak and maple trees into suitable logs for the wilp's central firepit; others were patching the holes in their salmon fishing nets. Young children were swimming in the warm-water ponds of the tributary streams. Adolescent children were assisting their parents, weaving rugs, carving totem poles, and sewing garments and boots for the predictable snows of winter. Smiles induced by the satisfaction of physical labor with a purpose seemed to accompany the energy required for the dawn-to-dusk efforts of the entire clan. Rest would come when zero-degree temperatures and the north wind penetrated the seams of the wilp's caribou-skin roofs and sides.

Summer and fall were also the favorite seasons for children when freedom of movement allowed them to explore the woods, streams, rocks, and caves near their backyards. They dreaded the dark, confined atmosphere of winter, when inactivity was the required expenditure of time. Spring, with the reappearance of buds, flowers, grass, birds, and spawning fish, was a welcome relief to the confined people of the river mist. The availability of outdoor activity was especially gratifying to young children, who found little to do in the dark, crowded confines of the wilp. Spring's arrival was especially welcome for those who were experiencing freedom of air and space for the first time in months. Such was the situation when child and dog joined in unrestricted physical activity after a winter of confinement.

Kwantum had a young puppy for his two-year-old sister, who was enjoying a new freedom of movement on her deerskin blanket. Agoni's introduction to Griffin exceeded Kwantum's expectations. Agoni had seen tethered dogs while riding in her cradleboard, but the meeting today was as personal as it could be. Lying on her blanket, Kwantum introduced Griffin to her. Griffin immediately accepted Agoni by vigorously licking her face and arms. Agoni seemed to understand Griffin's form of friendship. She smiled and reached out to him with both hands. At that point, Kwantum calmed Griffin's aggressive attempts to greet his new friend, bringing him sufficiently close for petting but free of the enthusiastic licking.

Friendship between Agoni and Griffin continued to grow. He was present each day as Kwantum played with Agoni on her blanket or when he carried her in his arms, which seemed to be the desired form of transportation for both. Griffin watched her learn to roll on her stomach, raise her chest off the rug, crawl, and finally pull herself to a standing position, ready to walk. He waited patiently as she acquired each phase of upright locomotion, his presence giving her the assurance that it was okay to try new ways to move. Agoni seemed to understand Griffin's concern because when she success-fully completed a new skill she looked to him for approval. Agoni and Griffin developed an association wherein Griffin's presence pro-vided the confidence Agoni needed in her new explorations. When successful, she looked to him as if to say, "See, I can do this now."

Bareback riding was a skill girl and dog developed without adult instruction. While Griffin was resting on the carpet, Agoni, now two years old, walked to him and climbed on his back, securing her seat by grasping handfuls of Griffin's long hair. Kicking both of her heels into his ribs, Griffin rose and carefully walked along the main path of the encampment. Dog and rider attracted the attention of adults and children along their journey. Agoni's grin and what also seemed to be a smile on Griffin's lips showed the joy each felt in their new adventure. When Griffin decided that Agoni had ridden enough, he returned to the carpet, laid down so she could dismount, and watched as she ran to tell Blue Cloud and Metonka of her new skill. Dog rides became a daily ritual, much to the joy of rider and dog.

Boys in the Eagle Clan were taught to be industrious at an early age. Kwantum's foster father, Blue Cloud, was an expert carver of totem poles, whose reputation had spread throughout the region, including the entire Pacific Coast north of Prince Rupert. Attempts to teach Kwantum the art of carving resulted in disinterest from his pupil, but the weaving skills of his mother were fascinating. Using his hands in fine motor skills became Kwantum's occupational hobby, which also became a valuable domestic contribution.

His dexterity qualified as an occupational contribution when he noted that Agoni's feet were covered with scratches and scrapes due to constantly running barefoot in the meadows and trails of the encampment. He solved the problem by measuring her feet and then cutting and sewing ankle-length moccasins, made from an otter skin he had trapped that fall. The black, smooth, shiny moccasins were an immediate trophy for Agoni, who wore them constantly and showed them to everyone she met, pointing and saying, "*Sak-sak*" (meaning *boots, boots*). She became so attached to the form-fitting footwear she refused to take them off at bedtime. Metonka solved the problem by removing the moccasins when Agoni was asleep.

The *gathering* requirement of the Eagle Clan each fall involved harvesting wild rice that grew in the meadows of numerous tributary streams flowing into the Skeena River. Kwantum demonstrated his ability to guide a birch bark canoe, which was the receptacle used to hold the rice as it was separated from its stalk, into the rice fields without disturbing the fragile stems. Expertise in using his paddle to sweep the rice into his canoe, instead of into the water, made harvesting rice his expected task each September.

On this sunny September day of rice harvesting, he had filled the canoe to its capacity, guiding the canoe to a place where the stream entered the Skeena River, feeling proud of his unique skill. Rice was an essential staple in the clan's winter diet. Near his encampment, he became aware that many of the adults were waiting for him. He safely beached his loaded canoe and then learned why his family and neighbors appeared to be concerned.

"Where are Agoni and Griffin? We have looked everywhere in the camp, so we thought they were with you," said Metonka.

"They were playing near the wilp when I left this morning," said Kwantum. "I haven't seen them since."

He was relieved that Griffin was also missing. Leaving the unloading of the rice to the gathered crowd, he hurried to the trail on which he, Agoni, and Griffin had walked several days ago. Agoni enjoyed the venture, especially the part where she could ride on Griffin's back. Kwantum knew there were no other places where she and Griffin could have gone, once the area surrounding the cleared portion of the encampment had been searched.

He sped along the earthen trail, encouraged to see Griffin's footprints, with their five sharp claws, distinctly different from those of a wolf or coyote. Frequently, the footprints became larger and more distinct.

"Aha," exclaimed Kwantum. "Agoni is riding Griffin's back."

He did not call or whistle, fearing Griffin would respond to the sound and thereby leave Agoni momentarily alone. Tracks continued along the main trail, ignoring the many smaller detours that large and small animals had used for centuries. At a bend in the trail, his intuition was rewarded. There, in a small space off the main trail, lay Griffin, with Agoni fast asleep, using his body as a pillow. Dog and girl were nearly two miles from the encampment, suggesting that Agoni had ridden Griffin for much of the distance. Kwantum awakened Agoni, but she did not seem to view the adventure as anything unusual. She walked and rode intermittently on their return to the encampment, chatting innocently about everyday life as viewed by a two-year-old girl.

Griffin's companionship with Agoni was frequently interrupted because of his newfound talent. When big game animals such as caribou and moose were shot and field dressed, their entire carcasses were transported to the encampment. Whole animals, including hooves and antlers, were rendered for some useful purpose. Transporting the large carcasses across marshes, over hills, and through dense forests required unusual amounts of energy. In northern British Columbia, this energy was routinely provided by the ingenious combination of dogs hitched to a sled made of caribou hides.

Sled dogs were tethered at the outskirts of the hunting area until they were called by the hunter. Griffin was included in the three-dog team because of his strength and endurance. Finding the bagged game once again demonstrated his genealogy beyond that of his domestic cousins. Once the shot was fired, however distant or faint the sound, Griffin would get to his feet, thereby telling the teamster and the sleeping dogs that it was time to work. His instinctive selection of the most object-free and shortest path to and from the desired site was an uncanny sixth sense that most likely had been developed and refined over the centuries, while similar perceptions in domestic animals may have decayed from lack of stimulation and necessity.

Griffin's first-tandem position as a sled dog was determined because he was larger and stronger than his teammates. Blue Cloud often used the five-tandem team when he traveled along the frozen Skeena River to Hazelton for supplies. Today, he decided to shorten the journey by crossing one of the numerous ponds formed by the tributary streams that flowed into the river. The team was about to enter the pond when Griffin balked, bracing his front paws against the frozen ground, thereby halting the entire team. Blue Cloud, as teamster, viewed the maneuver as disobedience and immediately chastised Griffin by stinging him with his long whip. With the crack of the whip, Griffin ceased his resistance and moved ahead with the team.

In the middle of the pond, the ice gave way and the entire team, sled, and teamster found themselves in six feet of water. Blue Cloud, with his enormous strength, swam to the trace line and cut it, thereby freeing the dogs, which had been imprisoned by the submerged sled, so they could swim and run to safety. Blue Cloud, although encumbered with soaked deerskin clothes, also managed to reach safety on the bank, where vigorous exercise rid him of his icy covering. Calls for assistance were answered by a neighboring clansman, allowing him to seek shelter in his friend's wilp. A change of clothes and a cup of soup fortified him for the two-hour walk to his wilp. True to neighborly tradition, Chief Nacon ordered his most reliable teamster to harness dogs and transport Blue Cloud to his home. The sled remained submerged until the warmer waters of summer allowed for its retrieval.

The dogs had been curried and fed when Blue Cloud called Griffin, petted his head, and said, "I am sorry, Griffin. I will never question your judgment again. From now on, you will be my lead dog. You were wiser than all of us. How did you know the ice was unsafe?" Once again, Griffin's genealogy, honed by centuries of survival, had expressed itself in a situation far removed from actual experience.

Agoni becomes a musher. Training and fitness of sled dogs was a required task of the clan's teamsters. The arrival of Blue Cloud as an Eagle Clan member solved the recurring problem. Blue Cloud possessed an unusual talent for working with sled dogs, which represented the clan's only rapid form of transportation when deep snow prohibited any other form of locomotion. Training the dogs was a year-round task, which was a disagreeable chore until Blue Cloud joined the clan. He quickly assumed the responsibility of summer training, which occurred on the sandy plains behind the encampment.

As a training device, the dogs pulled a sled made of caribou hides, loaded with a large maple log as ballast. Dogs were expected to pull the sled in a circle, culminating with directions from the teamster for the team to pull the sled between two cedar posts, spaced eight feet apart. Dogs were trained to change directions by responding to the universal commands used to train animals such as horses, mules, oxen, and dogs. The verbal command of "Gee" meant "Go left," "Haw" meant "Go right," "Mush" meant "Move forward," and "Whoa" meant "Stop." Repetitions of the commands meant "Do more of the same."

Blue Cloud was busy training his dog team when they were joined by Agoni, who asked, "Me drive?"

Her doting father agreed to her request by removing the maple log and placing her on the sled, having her grasp the two upright bars that were fastened by inserting cedar stakes into the caribou hide. He alerted the dog team for action and then whispered commands to Agoni, who shouted them to the dogs. The team seemed to understand that they were responding to a young driver, so they pulled the sled slowly and steadily as ordered by the faint, unfamiliar voice.

Blue Cloud stopped the experiment when they completed the circuit, allowing Agoni to step from the sled. She was not finished with her role as a teamstress, going to each dog, petting its head, and saying, "Good dog, Riley. Good dog, Jack," until she had thanked every dog. She looked at Blue Cloud with her affectionate smile, then turned and ran to her abode, telling Metonka, "Me mush, mush." Metonka had witnessed the entire event from a distance, so she smiled her approval, with a hug for Agoni, and a self-reminder not to be surprised at the antics of her precocious daughter.

Encampments surrounded by water were a signal that all children should learn to swim. River water was too cold and swift for young swimmers. The summer sun had warmed the water in pools of the meadows, making them inviting places to practice this essential skill in safety. Metonka and Kwantum agreed to take the five- to eight-year-old children for a swimming lesson. Both chaperones were excellent swimmers and were familiar with the rudimentary skills needed by beginning swimmers.

Demonstrations and practice were underway when Metonka noted that Agoni was not in the group of six students. She quietly stopped her demonstration, and motioned for Kwantum to assume the teaching, while she moved along the side of the pool beyond the site of the swimming lesson. She expected to see Agoni playing there, but she was not visible where Metonka had expected to see her. To her amazement, she saw Agoni's head emerge from the water, shake her wet hair, and begin a submerged swim to the other side of the pool, moving underwater until shortness of breath forced her head to reappear. When she saw Metonka, she did not appear to realize the anxiety her absence had caused. Apparently, the pace of the lessons occurred too slowly for Agoni's need to move in the water.

"Swim like fish," she proudly said.

Her mother led her back to the instructional site and demonstrated the crawl stroke, which she quickly learned was an efficient substitute for her underwater motions.

Harvesting and hunting had been completed by the second moon of fall. Chief Waban inspected the harvested grains, meat, and fish. He declared that the supplies were adequate for the clan's winter survival. He noted to Blue Cloud, who accompanied him on the inspection tour, "We have enough jerky from salmon. Venison from caribou and elk jerky are there in the meadows. We did not pick enough blueberries, blackberries, or currants, but we have plenty of rice, acorns, and hickory nuts. Next time you go to Hazelton for supplies, ask Agent Blackstone to include canned potatoes, corn, peas, and beans. If he can do that, we will be ready for winter."

Chief Waban's approval signaled the beginning of festivals to be held in the wilp. Celebration began with the harvest dance, performed by the men of the clan, involving males aged fourteen and older. Girls and women sat in a circle, watching the dancers perform to the beat of a tom-tom. With Blue Cloud as the lead dancer, they expressed thanks for the various types of food gathered, the fish caught, and the meat, now dried as jerky. Men danced in a counter-clockwise circle around the large fire, increasing the intensity of their chanting and physical expressions.

Agoni entered the circle of dancing men, with her little moccasin feet stepping, stamping, hopping, jumping, and twirling in perfect cadence with the beat of the drum. The men opened a space in the circle, allowing her room to dance. All had surprised smiles as they watched the graceful motion of the little dancer imitating their movements, and at the same time, making their actions look clumsy in comparison. Blue Cloud's masked smile told of his pleasure. His daughter performed the dance, which was new to her, but more expressive than his, who had led the dancers many times.

Agoni completed three circles around the fire, then left the dancers and sat by her mother. With a smile on her face, she seemed to say, "There! Girls and women can dance as well as men." Every eye in the wilp had seen the beautiful performance. In most societies, the exhibition would have evoked a standing ovation, but in this stoic audience, there was no visible recognition that such an unusual achievement had occurred.

28

Fig. 4 Kwantum, age eleven, and Griffin, age two years

Kwantum Attains *Manhood*

Overhead rays of the sun told Kwantum it was time to test his new venture. His mission began by pushing the bow of his eighteen-foot canoe into the rapidly flowing current of the Skeena River. His handcrafted canoe had an interior made of cedar staves; its exterior was covered with strips of birch bark, sewn together with elk sinews. The seams of the lightweight craft were waterproofed with a pitch from the red cedar trees that grew in abundance along the shores of the river. Kwantum had selected the fragile craft instead of the heavier, larger cedar canoes made famous by his ancestors because the birchbark canoe was easier for one person to propel through the river's swift current. His destination this sunny August afternoon was a smooth stretch of water below the Wrangle Falls, five miles from the permanent encampment of the Gitxsan Eagle Clan.

Kwantum's family summer residence was a small shelter built from red cedar posts, with the roof and sides covered with the branches of Norway pine trees and caribou hides. The permanent enclave of Kwantum's Clan was situated in a large cove, where the bend in the river had left an elevated, sandy plain, protected from westward rain and snow by outcroppings of overhanging rocks. Space was available for numerous wooden-built lodges, and most importantly, an ample area for the clan's wilp, a longhouse, where all members of the clan spent the cold, snowy months of winter.

Males of Kwantum's age were viewed as adults, with responsibilities for the procurement and storage of food for the clan. Today, his quest was salmon, a protein staple for the clan, and a major source of food for the numerous dogs that were needed for travel by sled when snow prevented any other form of transportation in the Skeena Valley. Several weeks ago, in preparation for his task, Kwantum traveled downriver to the Wrangle Falls—a five-foot impediment in the salmons' migration to their spawning area. A shallow bay below the falls was a temporary resting place for salmon before their attempted leap to the next level of their journey. Wrangle Bay was also a favorite fishing spot for grizzly bears, which sought the fat of the migrating fish as stored sustenance for their upcoming hibernation.

Watchful for camouflaged danger, Kwantum successfully navigated the currents of the river, skillfully avoiding places where submerged branches of fallen trees could tear large gaps in the fragile birchbark covering of his canoe. Upon completing his journey, he eased the bow of his canoe onto the grass-covered bank above the falls, anxiously looking to see if his trap was intact. He purposely kept the point of the wedge-shaped trap open so that, in his absence, salmon could freely exit the structure. Later this afternoon, he would push cedar staves between the existing passageways, thus trapping the northbound salmon that entered the enclosure during the night.

Kwantum's shelter tonight was a space next to the trunk of a large Norway spruce tree, its overhanging branches reaching the ground, providing 360 degrees of protection from wind and rain. His evening nourishment consisted of the cool, clean water of the river and half a filet of salmon jerky that he carried in his otter skin leather pouch. He shared the other half of his evening meal with Griffin, who seemed to enjoy his new adventure. Pine and spruce needles for a bed ensured that the fisherman and his companion would sleep in comfort.

Griffin's growl awakened Kwantum, indicating that something, most likely an animal, had alerted his keen senses of smell and hearing. The hair on his neck bristled, indicating that the cause of anxiety most likely was a bear. Kwantum did not bring his rifle, assuming that at this time of year, Griffin was all the protection he needed. August was too early for grizzly bears to be aggressive. Black bears that roamed the area were not likely to attack a human being unless provoked.

Morning sun appeared over the tops of the Sitka spruce that occupied the upper range of the rugged Babine Mountains. Kwantum parted the boughs of their nightly residence and stared in amazement. In the middle of the shallow pool where he had placed the trap, he saw seven adult grizzly bears, busily chasing and devouring the northbound salmon that had either just arrived at the pool or had attempted and failed to navigate the falls.

The presence of hungry bears in the wedged portion of Kwantum's trap caused numerous whirlpools, created by the frenzied splashing of trapped salmon. Their journey against the strong current of the Skeena River had thus far been unchallenging for the adult, twelve- to fifteen-pound fish. Their four-hundred-mile pilgrimage from the Pacific Ocean to their spawning grounds had been uneventful until they were confronted with the impediment of Wrangle Falls. Their first-ever encounter with grizzly bears, combined with the unseen and unexpected obstruction of the trap, was beyond the innate, elusive capability of the distraught fish, making their attempts to swim upstream an easy meal for hungry bears.

His hillside view allowed Kwantum to watch the excitement occurring around his trap, momentarily uncertain of his next action. With the instincts of a hunter, characteristic of his lineage, he went to his canoe, which was beached on the opposite side of the river from his trap, and thrust it into the river. He placed Griffin on the bow of the craft and paddled directly toward the bears. His shouting was muffled by Griffin's barking, but the combined clamor had its desired effect. An approaching canoe, with the flailing arms of the human and the excited barking of Griffin, caused the frightened bears to scurry into the wooded area beyond the banks of the river, leaving the trapped salmon for Kwantum's acquisition.

Seizing the opportunity afforded by a now-liberated pool, Kwantum placed his canoe at the side of the trap, within easy reach of the floundering salmon. With his net, made from narrow strands of caribou hide, suspended from the forked limb of an elm tree, he quickly scooped the squirming salmon into his canoe until their weight brought its gunwales to several inches above the water. He pulled the nearest stakes of the trap, thus allowing the remaining fish to reenter the river. Realizing that the bears would soon return for their interrupted meal, he guided his canoe and cargo of salmon across the pool, into a tributary stream that flowed parallel to the river.

When his canoe reached a point beyond the falls, Kwantum got out, pulled his loaded canoe across a short, grassy egress into the current of the river, then paddled against the current for the anticipated six-hour journey to his encampment. A successful fishing trip, with its possibilities of potential danger, was an example of the daily challenges faced by members of the Eagle Clan. Despite the rigors of their wayfaring lifestyle, they vigorously resisted attempts by tribes and organizations that sought to change their accustomed way of life.

Their arrival late that evening was greeted with cheers and congratulations. The apprehended salmon signaled that the clan's winter source of food had arrived and was available, paving the way for numerous clansmen with larger canoes to travel downriver for similar catches. Navigating the five-foot falls with a canoe filled with salmon had been an insurmountable obstacle until Kwantum discovered the tributary stream that circumvented the falls. Thereafter, Kwantum was allowed to sit with the men during their daily discussions that dictated the clan's activities—a significant gesture of maturity that ensured Kwantum's role as a voting member of the clan.

Fig. 5 Children ready to board train for Prince Rupert

Grim News from Agent Blackstone

Kwantum's joyous return from his fishing experience ended when he was drawn aside to receive a message from Chief Waban. Earlier that day, an assistant to Factor McKensey had arrived with a telegram from the governmental office in Prince Rupert containing a disturbing regulation pertaining to all Gitxsan children. Under a new order, each clan must submit half of their children for education in English schools. Based on the Eagle Clan's population, ten of their young children would be taken to a residential school for extended periods of time. Re-location would take place on August 20, merely a week from today. Younger children were preferable to fill the quota because of their presumed greater accommodation to changes in their established lifestyles.

Earlier in his role, Chief Waban would have vigorously resisted the government's order, but now his age and declining health had weakened his resolve. Inducements of food, blankets, guns, ammunition, and especially alcohol, to which he had become addicted, offered as incentives for compliance, were decisive factors. Despite what he knew would be strong objections from his Eagle Clan members, Chief Waban accepted the terms of the Factor's solution to the order. Gitxsan culture entrusted their chief with responsibility for all decisions regarding the welfare and education of their children. Once the decision was made, it was up to the clan members to embrace the verdict and endure its potential consequences.

The directive to remove children from their homes was more difficult than any the Eagle Clan had ever faced. Former Chief Grey Eagle moved the clan eighty miles upstream to avoid the very order that Chief Waban now accepted. Selection of who would be chosen to attend the residential school immersed the clan in serious debate.

Parents of all eligible children, those between ages five and fourteen, vigorously opposed the decision, but according to Gitxsan tradition, the Chief's commitment involved the clan's honor and therefore must be obeyed.

Chief Waban listened to parents' reasons why their children should not be sent to the residential school. After the members had spoken, he announced his decision. All five- and six-year-old children of the Eagle Clan would be included in the dislodgement, constituting the required quota of ten children. Younger children were selected, according to Chief Waban, because they were playmates and therefore would have companions at the school, and the selection of younger children complied with Factor McKensey's request. With his lack of comprehension, Chief Waban unwittingly ordered exactly what the Canadian government requested of its First Nations citizens. Several months from now, Chief Waban would realize the tragic consequences of his decision.

Blue Cloud was visibly displeased with the Chief's decision. As Captain of the clan's Territorial Patrol, he ordered his ten warriors to launch their canoes and travel to Hazelton to confront Agent Blackstone. Armed with rifles, the men completed the journey to Hazelton in record time. Four hours later, they were in Agent Blackstone's office, demanding an explanation involving the Factor's interpretation of the order.

Agent Blackstone, visibly shaken by the armed confrontation of his resident clan, asked the men to sit on the adjoining hillside while he explained the governmental order and how it was to be addressed. In appeasement, he offered to accompany the conscripted children to Prince Rupert and stay with them until they had safely boarded a train to their assigned residential school. His naïve impression was that the children would be enrolled in one of the newly formed residential schools near Prince Rupert. Governmental and religious leaders were aware of Gitxsan opposition to alien regulations and had included this resistance in their plan for the Gitxsan children.

Realizing that disobeying the government's order would have severe economic and territorial consequences, Blue Cloud knew that he had no alternative. His long-standing opposition to the acceptance of "free" food and supplies from the government was an inducement for Gitxsan people to sign treaties in exchange for land. Innovations that improved the lifestyle of his people, including axes, saws, hammers, posthole diggers, cooking utensils, pots, kettles, cups, plates, and dippers, had been earned by trading. Merchants on the Pacific Coast were eager to exchange European goods for furs, clothing, carvings, and blankets produced by the Eagle Clan members. He was aware that discipline associated with hard work in exchange for subsistence was being dissipated by sloth. Young clan members found it more convenient to search for stored items in the clan's dugout than to look for them in the hills and valleys of Skeena Valley.

Faced with the urgency of providing for the children's welfare, the problem of clan self-sufficiency would be addressed later. He would accept the order, with three conditions: that Agent Blackstone not only accompany the children to Prince Rupert but also ensure that they would be enrolled as a group and assigned to the same residential school; that one fourteen-year-old boy would be among the young children as a confidence builder (This condition was demanded by Blue Cloud because Agoni was the only five-year-old child in the group. Kwantum would be there to protect her.); and that Agent Blackstone must accompany the children to the residential school and reside there until he was satisfied that all were comfortably situated in their new environment.

Reflecting on Blue Cloud's demands, Agent Blackstone now realized how naïve members of the Eagle Clan were about the government's reason for mandating residential schools. Given his present predicament, he did not have the option of outright refusal to Blue Cloud's request, so he asked for permission to convey, via telegraph, the request to Factor McKensey, his immediate superior in Prince Rupert.

Agent Blackstone, equally conversant with the Gitxsan and English languages, knew that Blue Cloud's conditions were not likely to be accepted by Factor McKensey, but his dire situation allowed no other option but to place the request before governmental authorities. Agent Blackstone's transmission of Blue Cloud's demands to Factor McKensey received the expected response.

Hearing Agent Blackstone's reason, he replied, "Those insolent savages! What right do they have to question these orders? But, to move on, tell them you will accompany the children to their assigned school. I will send a replacement for you while you are away, and after a week the whole episode will blow over. Make sure that news of this situation does not reach Ottawa." The Factor had been assigned to Prince Rupert against his will, but he knew his only chance of reassignment was to receive a glowing report of compliance from the Inspector General.

Agent Blackstone conveyed the Factor's acceptance of Blue Cloud's demands to the waiting Territorial Patrol. He knew that boarding the train to the children's assigned school would end his authority to lobby for their welfare. He was also familiar with the authoritarian attitude of religious leaders, who envisioned their role as a God-given authority to intervene in the lives of Indigenous children. Their mission was to eradicate the *Indian culture*, despite the potential negative effects of this effort on the mental, physical, and emotional welfare of its recipients.

The Territorial Patrol's return to their encampment caused Agent Blackstone remorse and guilt for his role in facilitating the life-changing experience that he knew the children were about to encounter. His own experience as a child of mixed cultures had solidified his inherent opinion that the culture of the Gitxsan nation was genuine, legal, and sustainable, and therefore should be exempt from existing orders. Canadian governmental officials were clearly mistaken about the welfare of Gitxsan children in his area of responsibility.

The return of the Territorial Patrol set off immediate changes to the long-standing routines of the Eagle Clan. How would the members of the Territorial Patrol explain the upcoming exodus to the parents and children of those chosen for deployment? How could parents prepare their children for such a drastic change in their established, stable, and secure way of life? What changes could the children who were chosen expect? Who would teach them? How long would they be gone? Would parents be able to visit their children? Answers to questions facing the clan had deliberately been vague or unanswered, for fear that honest answers would increase resistance by the Gitxsan nation.

Optimistic views of those who eagerly sought to impose a provincial and religious culture on children in residential schools were strengthened by a compulsive resolve to obliterate the *Indian lifestyle* in exchange for a healthy secular and religious existence. Successful enrollment of Gitxsan children, whose parents had previously resisted any attempts of interference in their independence, was viewed as a decisive victory for the government, and by religious organizations, an opportunity to save souls.

Life in the Eagle Clan on deployment day for the five- to six-year-old children was tense and contentious. Members of the clan would eagerly have taken up arms against those who were responsible for the imposed removal of children. A combination of tribal custom and the cooler heads of Chief Waban and Blue Cloud were needed to arrange for the orderly transportation of children, via canoe, to Hazelton.

At noon on the appointed day, five wooden canoes, each containing two adults and two children, entered the Skeena River for the eighty-mile journey. Farewells, according to Gitxsan culture, were without any visible show of emotion, but sadness was visible on the faces of parents, and despite the tradition of stoicism, many of the children were convulsed with tears. In their young lives, none had ever been separated from parents or grandparents. Being told that the upcoming journey would be long and without any family members present was an inconceivable arrangement.

Swift currents of the Skeena River sped the lightly laden canoes to Hazelton in sufficient time to meet the 4:00 p.m. arrival of the Western Pacific train, which had begun its westward journey from Ottawa four days ago. Its dual purpose for traveling west was to transport food, fuel, and machinery to the numerous stations in the Midwest and Mountain states. Four of its cars were reserved for passengers; cars which shortly would transport the school-bound children to Prince Rupert.

Arrival at the depot was the first novelty of the day for the new arrivals. They had never seen large wooden buildings such as the military commissary. Steel railroad tracks in front of the building served as amazing walking beams, on which they practiced their balancing skills. The sound of the train's whistle, combined with the now visible approaching train, was another source of amazement. They had heard the train's whistle on the wings of a south wind from their encampment, but now they saw its source—a large, black monster that seemed to stretch on forever. Momentarily, their anxiety turned to astonishment and then to wonder when they were told they would ride on the train that afternoon.

Conductor Alby seemed to be in a hurry as he motioned the children to the steps of a waiting car. Little time to say farewell was allowed for the parents who had taken them to the station. They climbed onto the large, cushioned seats, the whistle blew, and the train began to move. The children had ridden in a canoe, but this type of movement was different. Trees whizzed by with amazing speed, and the rails provided a smooth ride, faster than their young minds could imagine. So engaged were they with the rapidly moving train that the eighty-mile ride to Prince Rupert was completed before any of them realized where they were going and what to expect when they arrived. Thoughts of separation from their parents had diminished, nor did they have any idea that the government intended their exciting journey to be the beginning of a deployment lasting for years—long enough to erase any memories of ever having been an Indian.

The slowing speed of the train and its whistle alerted the children that another new experience awaited them. "We're in Prince Rupert," announced the conductor, in a voice that the children surmised must have been spoken in English, but which none of them understood. Kwantum could tell by the actions of the passengers that it was time to leave the train. In their native language, he told the children to follow him—a direction which had just been given to him by government agent Mrs. Atkins. They followed Mrs. Atkins to a room at the rear of the station, where they were, by hand motions, told to sit on the large chairs that filled the room. She was soon joined by several men, each carrying a flat, black object in his hands that, when opened, contained pieces as thin as leaves.

"What do we have here?" asked one who appeared to be the oldest of the group.

"These children are here to fill the quota for the Gitxsan Eagle Clan," answered Mrs. Atkins.

"That will be a challenge," replied the man. "The Gitxsan are an independent group. They have given us trouble in the past."

"They will not this time. Look at how young they are. Once we get them to the school, they will be easy to train," replied the second man. "They will forget that they were Indians. Ms. Crosswhite will have them speaking English in a month."

Factor McKensey entered the room and informed the four adults that the children had been assigned to Kamloops Residential School. They would spend the night in the train depot, where they would eat supper and sleep on the floor, using their caribou robes as blankets. The next morning, they would board a schooner to be taken to Kamloops. Kamloops Residential School had been chosen because of its distance from the Eagle Clan's encampment, thus reducing the possibility of visitations from the children's parents. Agent Blackstone's appeal to enroll the children in a school near their home was not considered a possible option. Gitxsan's resistance to forced assimilation was a major reason for the selection of a school not easily accessible by visiting parents or runaway enrollees.

Morning produced additional surprises for the children, who were already overwhelmed by the events of the previous day. Awakened by the depot matron, they were taken to separate, small rooms. Toilet requirements were met by asking the girls to sit on what appeared to be a hard, white, cold stool, which was more comfortable than sitting on parallel logs in their encampment. Afterward, they were taken to a large room filled with tables and chairs—chairs on which the children climbed to reach the food that had been placed in separate spaces on the table.

The food was a combination of what looked like their porridge, topped with strawberries that were four times larger than the ones that grew along the hillsides of the Babine Mountains. The fluid in the metal cups was called milk, which tasted better than the water they drank at home. Milk looked like the kind that puppies got from their mothers before they could eat big people's food, but they had never seen cows, so they wondered how so much milk was available. Thus far, the food provided by the white squaws was good, especially tasty because they were hungry and had not been allowed to help themselves to the family porridge that was always available in the wilp.

After breakfast, the children were escorted to the dock, where a *large canoe* was waiting to take them to a city called Kamloops. They were told to climb on the large seats and wait for the schooner to move. Empty seats soon filled with people who wore clothes the children saw for the first time. Some men wore head coverings that stood high above their heads—the kind that would not stay on long in the low-hanging branches of the forest. Women carried small bags made of tanned fur from animals, like those their fathers may have caught. Women wore dresses with large flowers on them, like the pictures that their mothers placed on tanned deerskins, using black and red dyes.

A loud horn was a sign that the *big canoe* was about to move, without anybody paddling it. Soon it was moving nearly as fast as the train they had ridden the day before. To the right side of the *canoe*, there was water as far as they could see. Many other *canoes* were on the water—some of them carried many people, who stood on the sides as other *canoes* moved past them. Houses and large buildings were all along the shore. Some of the *canoes* had houses on them. After a long ride, they moved into a row of posts with smooth wooden boards called docks.

Tying the *canoe* to some posts, the children were told to follow a man who took them to a sled with wheels, pulled by two animals larger than a moose, called horses, who were tame and obeyed the man who sat on a seat behind them. When the children were seated on benches that were on both sides of the wagon, the man told the horses to move along a wide trail, called a road. They came to a large, white building, which, the driver told Kwantum, would be their home for a long time. The horses stopped in front of the building called a school, where the driver got off the wagon seat and tied the horses to a post.

"Follow me," he said, as he walked into an opening in the front of the building. "Ms. Crosswhite will take care of you now." He went back to the horses and drove away. They learned the sled with wheels was called a taxi, used to bring and take people to the docks for rides on the train or schooner.

Fig. 6 Residential school

Turmoil in the Residential School

"Come in," said the woman who sat behind a large table, called a desk. She told the many women helpers to each take ten of the children to separate places in the large room and wait there until she called them. Children of the Eagle Clan were intentionally dispersed so that none was in a group of familiar faces. Agoni was frightened, but she could see her friends in the various groups, which momentarily reduced her anxiety. She also recognized the faces of children from other clans, with whom she had played during the social potlatches. Perhaps the new school would be more fun than it appeared in her first impression.

"We are going to give you new White person's names," said Ms. Crosswhite, whose need for power demanded that she also control the naming process. "The names that you have do not fit into your new world. You will be sent to me, one by one, to hear your new name."

Seated near Ms. Crosswhite's desk were three women with machines that poked thread into cloth. As Ms. Crosswhite pronounced the child's new name, each seamstress sewed the name several times on a strip of cloth. The strip with names was then given to monitors, whose responsibility it was to separate the names and sew them, as a means of identification, to the children's various outer garments. The naming process continued without incident until it was Agoni's time to be renamed.

"What is your name?" asked Ms. Crosswhite.

"Agoni," answered the little girl.

"Well, let me see," said Ms. Crosswhite, as she moved her finger down a long sheet in a book that lay on her desk. "Here we are.

Maria! That will be your name. The first Maria left us yesterday, so now you will be the new Maria."

"No, no," shouted Agoni. "Name is Agoni. Agoni Blue Cloud."

"My, you are a little hellion. But you will break, and then you will be tame like the rest of them. Take her away, and be sure the tags are sewn on today."

As she was being led away, Agoni turned and shouted, "Agoni. Agoni Blue Cloud." The matron grasped her arm and led her to the next part of her orientation procedure.

"You, you, you," said the matron, as she pointed to the children standing before her. Motions of her hand seemed to say "Come with me," as children gathered around her. Similar groups were being formed by the other helpers until all the children were in groups of ten.

Agoni's group was led by a nice squaw, named June Ames, who spoke to them in Tsimshian—the parent language of all the tribes in British Columbia. It was the first time during the trip that an adult had spoken to them in other than the English language. What she told them caused unspeakable alarm. They were going to have their hair cut and then given clothes made of cloth. Each group, when called, was to follow their leader into separate rooms, where the indicated events would take place.

Cutting of hair occurred by placing the child on a high chair, where the child was draped by a large apron. A woman barber cut the children's hair—the procedure taking only minutes after they were seated. Cutting completed, she stretched the remaining hair with a long, slender stick, called a comb. Gitxsan children rarely combed their hair, but when they did, it was with the short, stubby twigs from the branch of a young cedar tree. The coarse hair of the Gitxsan children was difficult to comb because it was seldom combed, and hair required thinning for the White man's comb to pass through it. The trauma of combing hair was left to the children, who were each given a comb with which to practice their newly assigned task.

Agoni protested when it was her turn for a haircut, saying, "No cut hair. Must keep all hair." In Agoni's religion, girls' and women's hair was cut only when a close relative died. Mourning continued until the hair had reached its original length. Agoni, who had been gone from home for two days, wondered if one of her parents or grandparents had died. She did not understand that short hair was hygienically necessary in confined environments.

"John, Al," shouted the barber. Her call was answered by two maintenance personnel, who knew what was expected of them. They walked to Agoni, and with one on each side, placed the screaming, kicking girl on the high chair. Agoni continued her protests, making it impossible for the barber to safely cut her hair. Both men seemed to know what to do without further instructions. One held Agoni on the chair, while the other placed his hands on Agoni's head in a position for the barber to complete her task. She grasped Agoni's long braids and, one by one, severed them above shoulder length. Agoni had consumed all her energy in resistance, so when the barber said, "All done," she took her comb, jumped from the chair, ran to the corner of the room, where she sat, pulled her knees to her chest, and sobbed silently.

Haircutting completed, monitors were told to take the children to another room for fitting clothes. Agoni refused to leave her corner position until Teacher June approached her and, in Tsimshian, asked her to come with her. Hearing a voice that spoke a language she understood, she grasped June's hand and walked with her to the assigned room.

Entrance to the next room induced additional resistance from Agoni. She was told to take off all her clothes and place them in a wooden box. The matron went to a table filled with piles of clothes, the kind that Agoni had seen on other young people at the school. Items that were brought to her looked strange. She was told to watch other children get dressed and then do the same. She had never worn underwear or socks, and the leather shoes were stiff and tight. June persuaded her to wear her new clothes and see how well they fit. Agoni was unable to wear the tight-fitting shoes, so she carried them to her room, a place that she was told would be her home for a long time.

June told her group of ten to follow, holding Agoni's hand to ensure that all her pupils arrived at the assigned rooms. She said,

"These rooms will be where you stay while you visit us." She then motioned for five of the children to enter the first of two adjoining rooms and asked the remaining five, including Agoni, to enter the second room.

"Sit on a bed. This will be your own place. We will share this room, but each of you must stay in your place while you are in this room."

The children quickly went to a bed, leaving the one in the corner for Agoni. She had never slept on a mattress—a soft straw called wool, covered with cloth. Her favorite sleeping habit had been to curl up in her caribou robe and lie on the ground floor of the wilp. Having such a large place to herself, lying on a long, thin board covered with a cloth over more straw—called a bed, and it too was covered with a soft, thick cloth—was fantastic. Lying on the bed was strange but a wonderfully comfortable feeling. She was tired and ready to sleep, but June told the children it was time to eat.

The children had not eaten since noon, so the meal, called supper, was a welcome finish to a hectic day. They entered a large room with tables and benches. Many children stood behind the benches. Agoni was so hungry she sat down and began to eat, as her clan ate in the wilp. Immediately, a matron grasped her arm and, pulling her up, said, "Stand up. Here we pray before we eat. Because you disrespected God, tonight you will stand while you eat."

Supper consisted of oatmeal in a metal bowl, mixed with milk and honey. Bread and water were on the table for the children to consume as they pleased. Eating the porridge with a spoon while standing was difficult. When the matron came to clean the table, Agoni received her second scolding.

"My, what a messy child you are," she said.

Seeing Agoni in tears, June came to her rescue, leading her to the newly assigned room, where Agoni climbed into her bed, not taking time to change into the strange sleeping clothes, which were new to all the children. June noticed that she was asleep as soon as she crept under the covers, so she did not insist that Agoni sleep in her new nightgown.

Schedules at the residential school followed a military pattern, originally proposed by Col. Pratt at the Carlisle Industrial School in Pennsylvania. Pratt's model for daily living was originally developed and implemented for adults, but the combination of inexperience, naiveté, and the zeal of religious organizations imposed this inappropriate lifestyle on conscripted children in Canada and the United States. The model existed for over a hundred years, despite evidence that the rigid work schedule, inadequate food, and physical and sexual abuse were detrimental to the growth and development of conscripted children.

Days at the residential school began with the sound of a steam-powered whistle, so shrill that no one in the school escaped its blast. At 5:30 a.m., children were expected to arise, get dressed, attend to their toilet needs, wash their hands and faces, clean their rooms, rearrange the bed covers, and, if time permitted, spend the remaining time in prayer. In fall, winter, and spring, the building was lighted by the dim, chimney-covered flames of kerosene lamps and lanterns. Lights, according to military precedent, were extinguished at 8:00 p.m., supported by the belief that children and adolescents required nine hours of sleep each day.

"Wake up. Time to greet the day," announced the matron in a language that none of the children understood. She opened the doors and hung the kerosene lantern from a hook in the ceiling. Children scurried to find their clothes in the semidarkness, seeking to locate their shoes instead of those belonging to their sleep mates. Toilet call was accomplished by twos until all had completed their required washing of hands and face, first in cold water and soap, and then in warm water. Faces were washed with cloths. Towels and facecloths were hung on the footrail of the bed, ready for use in the evening. Using a face cloth dipped in warm water was another new experience for the children. At home, they washed by splashing water on their faces and then allowing air to dry the wet skin.

Breakfast began with the sound of the same whistle that awakened them. Matrons escorted children to the large dining hall, where food had already been placed on the tables. While standing behind a bench, hands were folded as a member of the clergy recited a prayer.

The customary bowl of oatmeal and milk, supplemented with bread and butter, awaited the hungry children, who were required, military style, to finish their meal in a half-hour. Talking was not permitted, due to the necessity of feeding several hundred children during the ninety minutes allocated for meals.[2]

Religious instruction began at 8:00 a.m. on the first five workdays of the week. Lessons continued until 9:30 a.m., when the bored children were given a thirty-minute recess. English-style education continued at 10:00 a.m. and ended when the 12:00 p.m. whistle indicated it was time for the noon meal, called dinner. Meals were provided in a prearranged, predictable schedule, allowing children to forecast what would be served for each meal, depending on the day of the week.

Difficulty during the process of eradicating the children's heritage occurred when the missionaries attempted to convert them to the Christian faith. Catholic, Anglican, Methodist, and Presbyterian missionaries refused to acknowledge or ignore the chasm that exists between eradication and renewal. A belief that had been reinforced daily since childhood was likely to have immediate and long-term detrimental psychological and mental consequences during the process of eradication. Strong resistance was encountered when eradication of a strongly held belief was the educational objective, as exemplified by the instruction of Indigenous children. Instead of attempting to resurrect a previously held belief, as may have been the occasion for English- and French-speaking children in Eastern Canada, Indigenous children experienced eradication, then replacement by a foreign abstraction called Christianity.

Members of the Gitxsan Nation evoked religion in their everyday lives. Inherent belief in a Supreme Being was transferred to the permanent and predictable elements of their environment. Gods to which they prayed included the sun, stars, wind, rain, and water. Human beings, animals, and fish possessed spirits that had an eternal

---

[2] Established in 1893, the Kamloops Residential School acquired a peak enrollment of five hundred children. The school closed in 1978.

existence. Prayers consisted of petitions for guidance, assistance, and thanksgiving for benefits provided by specific gods.

Religious sessions at the residential school were conducted in the chapel—a source of pride for Ms. Crosswhite, who had been the chairperson of successful fundraising efforts that enabled the school to build an impressive, on-site chapel. Lessons were one hour in length, conducted by clergy and occasionally by Ms. Crosswhite, who, when not teaching, became a frequent supervisor and observer to assess the effectiveness of the intended conversion.

On this fateful day of worship, she allowed the five-, six-, and seven-year-old children to leave the chapel, but as Agoni was about to exit the building, she was stopped by Ms. Crosswhite.

"Maria, I did not see you kneel when you approached the altar, fold your hands when praying, and you did not make the cross on your chest before the prayer. Tell me why you refuse to do as you were taught. When you refuse to do this, you make God angry."

"God not dead," said Agoni, pointing to the crucifix in the front of the church.

"God, who is also Jesus, died so our sins are forgiven. He is alive, and in heaven now."

"Me not sin," answered Agoni.

"Yes, you are sinning now, by not doing what I ask of you. Because you have sinned, you are going to stay in the chapel so you can think about what you just said. There will be no recess for you today."

Sin, repentance, and forgiveness were strange concepts to Agoni. In her culture, persons whose actions or verbal expressions were contrary to the accepted protocol were shamed, isolated, and, in extreme situations, removed from the clan until corrective actions had occurred. Every action or thought of the clan members was related to the ancient concepts of sustenance and survival. The social structure of the clan ensured that every action or deed was observed and acknowledged. The clan's safety demanded that detrimental actions be addressed and changed immediately. Greed, slander, sloth, falsehoods, and any physical contact in anger were addressed and corrected immediately.

Agoni accepted her punishment, as she had so many times, unsure of why the white man's religion was so mean. Punishment seemed to be an ever-present component of learning.

At dinner time, Teacher June, ever observant about her students, noted that Agoni was not in line. "Where is Maria?" she asked Ms. Crosswhite, who was monitoring the children.

"She was stubborn and wouldn't do what I asked her to do, so I made her stay in the chapel so she could think about her behavior," said Ms. Crosswhite.

"It is cold in the chapel," exclaimed June Ames. "She'll freeze there!" Without waiting for any more words from Ms. Crosswhite, she hurried to the chapel. Her first observation concluded the chapel was empty. She walked to the front of the church, where she saw Agoni lying on the front pew, curled in a fetal position.

"Maria, wake up. It is time for dinner," said June.

"Cold, cold," said Agoni.

"I know. Here, wrap yourself in my coat. When you are warm, we will go and eat," said June.

With the warm coat, wrapped in the arms of June, Agoni stopped shivering and was soon ready to enter the dining room. However, the situation was so displeasing to June Ames that she decided to send a report to Director McLeod, recounting the numerous situations in which she felt children were being mistreated.

Afternoon classes for the five-, six-, and seven-year-old children were a continuation of nursery-style education, with an emphasis on the pronunciation and meaning of English words. Children were asked, in unison, to repeat words spoken by the teacher, reinforced with a limited supply of visual aids. Conversations between children were to be spoken in English, with punishments for those who were detected speaking their native tongue.

Recess time was the favorite time of the school day for the children—a release from the military-style education at the Kamloops Residential School. Five-, six-, and seven-year-old children had two recess times—the first from 9:30 to 10:00 a.m., and the second from 2:30 to 3:00 p.m. Playgrounds were large, with room for free play and space for equipment, which most of the children had never seen.

Agoni was attracted to what appeared to be a swing. At home, her swing was a strand from a wild grapevine that had climbed a tall hickory tree. Attached to a branch and severed from its roots, the vine hung freely, swinging in the wind. Children grasped the rope-like vine and ran until the vine carried them into the air. By grasping tightly, they could ride the vine far beyond its starting point and then jump off for a two-footed landing.

Six swings on the playground hung in a row, each with a leather seat attached to ropes which hung from a tall tree-like post, held upright by several metal posts. Agoni watched several of the children sit on the leather seat and push themselves back and forth. When it was Agoni's turn to have the swing, she sat down and began to run forward. When airborne, she flexed her knees to move the swing backward, then extended her knees to move the swing forward. After several back-and-forth movements, the swing was seven feet above the ground in its forward motion.

This was the moment Agoni was anticipating. When the swing reached its maximum forward motion, Agoni jumped, as she had always done when swinging from the grapevine. Playground monitors gasped when they saw Agoni flying, thinking she had lost her grasp on the ropes. Agoni landed on her feet and continued to run, without any sign of injury. The fun of what became known as swing-jumping intrigued the children, who tried to repeat Agoni's feat. However, none could land on their feet, resulting in bruises, scrapes, and several sprained ankles. Injuries alarmed the playground monitors, who declared there would be no more swing-jumping. Agoni's skill was noticed by maintenance personnel and Ms. Crosswhite, who grudgingly admitted that little "Maria" was an unusual athlete.

Kwantum's status as a preferential resident resulted from an incident while he was on a work detail, sweeping leaves from the walkway in front of the school. As he swept, he was struck by an errant soccer ball that escaped the team's soccer practice. He dropped his rake and, without any preparatory motion, kicked the ball, which sailed seventy yards—far beyond the expectations of waiting players, who watched the kick in admiration. None of the team members was able to kick the ball in the manner they had just witnessed. Kwantum's kicking ability was also seen by Coach Jones, who approached Kwantum with a request for him to join the team.

"I am here on a work detail so I can look after my little sister," answered Kwantum. "Ms. Crosswhite will not let me play soccer when there is work to be done."

"Don't worry about Ms. Crosswhite. I will ask Director McLeod to give you a reprieve from afternoon work, so you can attend practices. And if the rest of your skills are as good as your kicking, you will have a place on the residential school team. What is your name? I will call Director McLeod tonight. Ms. Crosswhite will tell you tomorrow about soccer practice."

Coach Jones loved the task that he was about to initiate. He was aware of the tension that existed between Ms. Crosswhite and Director McLeod. He knew of Director McLeod's love for soccer, so he was confident about the outcome of his request. He also knew the extent of Ms. Crosswhite's contention when she would be forced to excuse Kwantum for soccer practice—a sport that she considered a waste of energy because it was not used for God's purpose.

Kwantum's initiation to the soccer team exceeded everyone's expectations. Coach Jones was impressed that Kwantum was not only an excellent kicker and striker, but he was also the fastest player on the team. His ability to dribble and evade opponents while in a scoring position would improve an offense that had been ineffective. His ability to tackle without fouling was another much-needed defensive skill.

Team members welcomed Kwantum because of his skills but soon learned to appreciate his ready smile. He was willing to teach them techniques with which they were not familiar—skills that he learned while playing the original Gitxsan game, a combination of lacrosse, soccer, and football.

Kwantum's skill as a soccer player soon spread throughout the thirteen- to sixteen-year age group, where he became a sports celebrity. Adult males, many of whom had played soccer, came to watch Kwantum practice, during which he showed his prowess as a runner, dribbler, passer, and most importantly, his ability to outmaneuver the goalie and score points. His ability soon became known throughout the league. Inside the school boundaries, he was given special privileges, including supervision of boys his age or younger, during their daily work details.

Today, as his work crew was raking leaves near the playground, he heard someone call his name. He dropped his rake as he looked up to see the caller, whom he recognized as Agoni. Running swiftly, Agoni threw her arms around him, and he embraced her with similar affection.

"Home, home," she said. "Want go home."

"Yes, I will take you, but you must wait until the spring moon. Home is far away. We must wait until it is warm, so we can sleep outside as we go home." Kwantum knew that taking Agoni with him in the cold November weather would endanger her life. He also knew that they were currently being watched, and both he and Agoni would likely be punished.

He continued raking leaves but soon saw Mr. Crosswhite's secretary approaching. The students knew the secretary's presence meant she had been sent by Ms. Crosswhite. "Ms. Crosswhite wants to see you," she announced. "Follow me."

"I saw Agoni run to you," said Ms. Crosswhite. "Did you speak to her in English?"

"No. She does not understand English. She needed someone to love her, and I was the only one here who could give her what she needed. I had to tell her, in her own language, that she would be safe and get to like this place."

"Oh, no! She understands English. Now you have undone everything we taught her in the last two weeks. Both of you must be punished. Your punishment will be to take these records to Director McLeod. He lives five miles from here, so if you start out now, you will be able to get back before dark. You may go now, and let this be a lesson to you."

When Kwantum reported to soccer practice that afternoon, he told Coach Jones he could not stay because of his punishment from Ms. Crosswhite.

"That old bitch," said Coach Jones. "Stay at practice. I will saddle two horses, and Coach Nester will go with you after practice. He can hide the horses behind the bushes near Director McLeod's house, and no one will know what happened. We will soon have freezing rain. I have some new horse blankets that you can use as covers. They will keep you warm and dry."

Kwantum delivered the records, and the adventure went according to Coach Jones's plan. Kwantum thought about the event that evening and was thankful for Coach Jones's assistance in completing his errand. While Coach Nester and he were riding to Director McLeod's home, the predicted freezing rain began. The coats that had been provided by the government were not rainproof, so without horse blankets, he and Coach Nester would have been soaked. In addition, the leather shoes that had been issued were not suited for rain or snow. He remembered the warm, waterproof boots and leggings that he would have worn during similar conditions at home. In many situations, the Gitxsan way was much better than the ones to which they were being exposed at Kamloops.

Kwantum was again summoned to Ms. Crosswhite's office the next morning.

"Director McLeod told me that you brought the records to him last evening. I hope you thought about why you were told to walk in the cold rain last night."

Kwantum stood in silence, expecting to be told he could leave.

"Don't you have anything to say for yourself?" demanded Ms. Crosswhite. "Are you speechless? I thought we taught you how to speak in English."

"I did what I was told to do. May I go now?" said Kwantum.

"Yes, and next time try to remember why you are here."

Kwantum walked back to his room, thinking about his experiences during the last month. "They are trying to change us through punishment, which is exactly the opposite of the Gitxsan way. Punishment is the opposite feeling we should have when we are corrected."

Students of Teacher June were very successful when learning about their new culture. Trying to speak the sounds of letters that made new words was fun, and trying to speak in English so that friends could understand them became a hilarious game. The success of Teacher June's students was apparent to the other teachers, especially because the Gitxsan children were regarded as the most difficult to teach. June did not divulge her secret, which was to pronounce words in their forbidden native language, and then have them repeat the words in English. She knew that if Ms. Crosswhite learned of her method, she would enforce the ban on Indigenous expressions that now existed.

Using their native language, although forbidden, was frequently spoken when the children were out of hearing distance from adults. To avoid being detected while "acting like Indians," the children would softly mutter "Boo, Boo" whenever they saw an adult, besides Teacher June, approaching as they were having fun with their native language. On the playground, they frequently came to Teacher June for help with an English pronunciation they wished to use in their games.

Socially adept Agoni became a favorite playmate during recess periods.

"Me Agoni. What you?" she asked. "Want run-chase?"

The game of running and fleeing was once a source of survival, but in present Native societies, it had become a playground favorite. Agoni emerged as the most elusive player due to her speed and agility. When chased, she ran toward her playmates, making them easy *victims* for the chaser. Playmates often watched as Agoni, being chased, used her skills to outmaneuver any of those who sought to catch her.

Teaching methods used by Teacher June were copied by Agoni as a playground teacher. She had an unusual ability to translate her language into the English version—the version that children were to use whenever they spoke. The game of learning English on the playground began with Agoni pronouncing a word in Gitxsan and having the children answer in English. The winner was the child who came closest to the English word as Agoni had pronounced it in her Gitxsan accent. Playground monitors became accustomed to seeing Agoni surrounded by a group of children, laughing while having a class in communications on the playground.

Fig. 7 Ms. Crosswhite, superintendent of Kamloops Residential School

Kwantum's Revenge and Reprieve

Cold November days brought an end to the afternoon recess periods. Classrooms were now used for sedentary games, which brought the children into close contact for every minute of the day. Playing outside in cold weather was thought to induce colds, but confinement to small spaces was the purveyor of an even more dangerous germ. Tuberculosis had been a consistent problem in previous years. The first few days of November suggested this year would see similar infections. Lack of space, with five children in each small room, was a built-in incubator for the multitude of germs to which the Indigenous children had no immunity.

Children who coughed were told to cover their coughs, but the germs seemed to be everywhere. Indigenous children had never been exposed to tuberculosis and therefore were especially susceptible to it. Agoni, perhaps due to her social habits, was the first in her small room to cough continuously, which became so exhausting that she was excused from classes and confined to her room. Her cough seemed to consume her entire body as it attempted to rid itself of the noxious invader.

"Maria keeps calling for you," announced the nurse as Kwantum was about to retire for the night. "Come to see her, so she will get the sleep she needs."

Kwantum had not seen Agoni for several weeks due to Ms. Crosswhite's isolation policy. He hurriedly followed the nurse to Agoni's room, where he found her four roommates asleep, but Agoni lay with her arms over her head, coughing incessantly.

"Hi, Kwantum," she said. "I sick. Tell Mommy love her. Tell Daddy love him. Give Griffin hug. Love you, too. Very tired. Must sleep."

She closed her eyes when the nurse told Kwantum it was time for him to leave. "Maria is very tired. Tomorrow, we will move her to the infirmary, where she will get better care."

As Kwantum opened the door to leave, Agoni opened her eyes, raised her hand weakly to say goodnight. Kwantum followed the nurse back to his room, reflecting in anger on the terrible misunderstanding about his race that had brought him and his relatives to this situation. How could his people endure the world of the white man if this feeling against them continued?[3]

Kwantum was helping the farmer feed his cattle the next morning when he was summoned to Ms. Crosswhite's office.

"I called you to tell you that your sister, Maria, died shortly after you left her last night," announced Ms. Crosswhite in a matter-of-fact voice, devoid of any emotion.

Kwantum was saddened by the announcement, but visiting Agoni last evening told him she was very sick.

"We buried her this morning, along with two other children who died during the night. She looked so peaceful, lying in her deerskin jacket and leggings with fringes on them. We even found her braids in the storage box and placed them on her shoulders. Her classmates walked by her casket, touching her hands, and making the sign of the cross as they went by. Rev. Ryan conducted a requiem mass to ensure that her soul is safely in heaven."

"Well, don't you have anything to say?" asked Ms. Crosswhite. "You should be happy that she is with Jesus, and her pain is gone. She was so lucky that she was included in the Gitxsan bunch, who are well on their way to becoming Christians. She was making good progress in learning about our ways, but now she knows all about them."

"Why didn't you tell me about her funeral?" asked Kwantum. In the Gitxsan tradition, funerals were a cause for celebrating the life

---

[3] Records of the Catholic Diocese listed fifty graves at the Kamloops cemetery. An anthropologist, using ground-penetrating radar, estimated the Kamloops site contained the remains of two hundred individuals.

of the deceased. Funeral celebrations lasted three days, but mourning continued for months.

"We thought about you, but we knew how much you loved Maria. We wanted you to remember her as the lively little girl with a big smile and black hair. We thought that seeing her in the casket would not be a good way to remember her."

Kwantum's anger momentarily returned to his ancient legacy, where an eye-for-an-eye was the essence of survival, but he knew that the use of force directed at Ms. Crosswhite and the residential school system would not solve his or the children's problems. He would go home and let Blue Cloud and the Gitxsan nation deal with the source of the problem, which he blamed on the Canadian government for initiating the problem and religious organizations for its continuation.

Fig. 8 Blue Cloud, ready for reprisal

Blue Cloud's Response to Injustice

Kwantum resumed his duties as firekeeper that evening, but he was preoccupied with the nonchalant way in which Ms. Crosswhite and the members of the clergy had dealt with Agoni's passing. To him, the experience seemed to say, "Being dead with Jesus is better than being alive." He knew that Agoni's Gitxsan religion had been her source of comfort during life at the residential school. He was determined to expose the entire system of forceful change as an unacceptable process, especially when its victims were children.

One of his functions as firekeeper was to fill the numerous lanterns and lamps with kerosene, stored in large barrels in the tool shed. He poured the liquid, but he could not forget the appalling way in which his sister and the other young children had been treated. His anger seemed to intensify as he filled the lanterns. A combination of events resulted in a plan of action. He would burn the chapel, the place of Agoni's frequent punishments, and where attempts to exterminate her religious beliefs had been the most aggressive. Doing so would require an escape from the school, an action which he knew was necessary if his plan was to be successful.

He filled the water tanks, which were a necessary component of the steam heating system for the two-story school, and then went to the tool shed, where a two-gallon sprinkling can was stored. After filling the can with kerosene, he carried it to the chapel where he sprayed liberal amounts of the liquid on the altar, carpets that covered both sides of the church, and the center aisle. He planted a short candle into the soaked carpet at the entrance of the chapel, which he lit as he left. The wick of the candle would burn down to the carpet in an hour, by which time he would be at the boat docks in Kamloops. He had taken wire-cutting pliers from the tool shed, with which he would cut the strands of the wire fence that isolated the residential school from neighboring houses. The official entrance to the gated enclosure was guarded by a police officer, stationed there to prevent the very action Kwantum was about to attempt.

November's dark night was an excellent cover for Kwantum's intended path to the docks. Dim streetlights made it difficult for anyone to identify him if residents were still awake at this hour. Arrival at the boat docks occurred without recognition. There was no one in sight to guard the empty vessels. He found the schooner that made its daily run to Prince Rupert, opened the hatch to the storage area, and climbed in. The room was cold and stuffy, but it was the only way Kwantum could get to his destination without being detected. When an examination of the burned remains of the chapel did not reveal his skeleton, there would be an extensive search for him, the person who would be suspected of setting the fire.

Morning found the docks alive with stevedores, pilots, and passengers. Fortunately, there was sufficient space for additional baggage at the entrance of the hold, which added to his concealment. The chill in the schooner's interior disappeared when the boiler's heat reached sufficiency to propel the boat toward Prince Rupert.

Kwantum's next challenges also required concealment and a disguise. Arrival of the schooner in Prince Rupert would alert authorities, who would be watching for him. He stood near the gangplank, spotted an opening amidst a group of passengers, and walked among them. Pretending to be one of their children, he was able to exit without detection. Passengers were intent on retrieving their luggage, therefore paying no attention to him.

Kwantum's next agenda item on his three-part journey was to board the two-o'clock train for Hazelton. Finding an open boxcar was an easy task on a train that had delivered machinery and supplies on its journey to Prince Rupert. Hungry and thirsty, he could not risk exposure in a search for food, thus endangering his mission, which now seemed within reach.

Arrival at Hazelton allowed Kwantum to immediately seek Agent Blackstone's assistance.

"They're looking for you," reported Blackstone when he saw Kwantum. "They sent word by telegraph, posting a reward for your capture. Remember, I did not see you, and you did not see me."

Hearing Kwantum's explanation, he offered to host him for meals and overnight lodging. Kwantum appreciated the offer but declined lodging, after accepting a meal and sufficient food for the eighty-mile journey to his encampment. Even among friends at the depot, he did not feel safe until he was in the custody of the Eagle Clan.

Kwantum, exhausted physically and mentally from his two-day attempts to reach his home, began his long journey to the Eagle Clan's encampment. Agent Blackstone insisted that Kwantum accept food and shelter for another day, but Kwantum's fervent desire to deliver his message overpowered his need for sleep, so he thanked Agent Blackstone and set out for home that afternoon. By using the snowshoes and poles lent to him by Blackstone, he made excellent progress by traveling on the frozen surface of the Skeena River.

Several hours before sunset, Kwantum was alerted by the sound of barking dogs—the sound of happiness, as expressed by sled dogs when running at their accustomed pace. Minutes later, he saw Blue Cloud and his team of dogs. Meeting Kwantum surprised Blue Cloud, who had not expected to see him until the spring full moon. Father and son delayed their reunion momentarily while Griffin greeted his friend with excessive licks, in return for the hugs that Kwantum provided. Blue Cloud waited patiently while the expression of love between boy and dog continued.

He then asked, "Why are you here? Where is Agoni? You are walking as though you are about to collapse."

"I ran away from the school. I had to come home to see if you can do something to stop the awful things that are happening there," answered Kwantum. "Agoni died two days ago. Can I tell you what happened after we get home? I need rest before we talk."

"Get on the sled. I will turn around. When we are home, and you have eaten and rested, you can tell me what happened."

Without any more conversation, Kwantum collapsed into the sled. Blue Cloud attempted to turn northward, but Griffin refused

Blue Cloud's command. Instead, he continued to face Hazelton, the direction from which Kwantum had just appeared. He soon began to whine, lifting his nose in the air as if to get Agoni's scent. Both Kwantum and Blue Cloud understood Griffin's actions.

"He's looking for Agoni," said Kwantum. He went to Griffin, patted his head, and said, "Agoni is not coming. Agoni cannot come with us anymore." The tone of Kwantum's voice and the look on Blue Cloud's face told Griffin that something was wrong and that it involved Agoni. He lay on the snow with his head between his front paws, continuing to look toward Hazelton, as though time would bring Agoni back.

"Come," said Blue Cloud. "If we are to get home tonight, we will have to start now." He gave the command to turn the sled, and with Griffin in the lead, they traveled the remaining forty miles of the homeward trek in record time. By midnight, the travelers were tired but safely at the encampment. The dogs had been fed, and Kwantum was resting on his caribou robe in the wilp.

Blue Cloud sat next to Kwantum, and the remaining clan members were within hearing distance. Kwantum told of the horrible life that Agoni and the remainder of the clan's children were enduring. The school's religious leaders were attempting to change the children through examples of odd behavior, followed by frequent punishment when children did not respond to actions to which they were not accustomed and to speak words to gods that were contrary to their religious beliefs. Members of the clan listened in silence, but facial expressions showed their astonishment as Kwantum told of the children's experiences.

Kwantum finished talking. Blue Cloud arose, held up his hand to denote silence, and began pacing counterclockwise around the firepit. His lips were moving, so his clan knew that he was praying, although they could not hear his words. After several trips around the firepit, he stopped and addressed the members of the Territorial Patrol.

"Tomorrow, go to as many of the wilps as you can reach. Tell the chiefs what is happening to our children. Tell them to bring rifles, sleeping robes, and food for two days. They are to meet at Hazelton shortly after noon in two days. We will show the Factor and the people in Ottawa that the Gitxsan tribe will not obey orders that harm our children and take away our freedom."

Blue Cloud's order to the patrol members ended the meeting, but members of the clan returned to their areas of the wilp in somber moods. They had planned for war before, but fighting the government was new to them. Previous preparations involved leaving their encampment to seek shelter in the vast woods that surrounded their permanent home. This encounter involved an opponent with whom they were unfamiliar, and whose plan of attack was unknown.

Early the next morning, Blue Cloud and the patrol members set out, via laden canoes, for Hazelton to prepare for what Blue Cloud envisioned as a show of force to cause a change in governmental policy. He knew, from rumors that had reached Hazelton, government officials were eager to avoid any disturbance akin to the North-West Rebellion of 1885. If, by show of strength, the Gitxsan Nation could demonstrate their opposition to the removal of children to foreign locations, perhaps such opposition would convince the Commissioner of Indian Affairs in Ottawa to change his view about the effectiveness of his assimilation policy.[4]

Agent Blackstone expected the Eagle Clan to react with force to the news that Kwantum brought to them. At noon the following day, he saw Blue Cloud's patrol beach their canoes at the post commissary. He welcomed the patrol, eager to learn how he could assist them in whatever action Blue Cloud had devised. He was surprised to learn of the active role that was expected of him in the forthcoming negotiations. His ability to speak Gitxsan and English, with an appreciation for the Gitxsan cause, made him the logical choice to articulate the clan's cause for rebellion.

Patrol members unloaded their canoes and found lodging sites within the depot. Blue Cloud explained to them and Agent Blackstone the action he had set in motion for the next day. Agent Blackstone

---

[4] Sometimes known as the Riel Rebellion, officially the North-West Rebellion in 1885 was a violent insurgency by Métis natives against the Canadian Government in a dispute over land rights. After a series of skirmishes, governmental force prevailed. Louis Riel, leader of the Métis forces, was arrested, tried for treason, and hanged on November 16, 1885.

was to demand, via telegraph, that Factor McKenzie board the afternoon train and arrive in Hazelton at mid-afternoon the next day.

"Tell the factor if he is not on the train we will come for him, and if we have to come for him the ride from Price Rupert to Hazelton will not be pleasant," said Blue Cloud. "And send the same message to Director McLeod in Kamloops. He will know why he is getting the message. The escape of Kwantum from the residential school, and the passing of Agoni two days earlier will tell him why we want to see the factor in Hazelton."

Agent Blackstone hurriedly relayed the message that Blue Cloud had given him. He was also in charge of arranging food and lodging for Blue Cloud's patrol, taken from the provisions that were stored in the depot as part of the monthly distributions to the various clans. Ill-prepared to supply food and lodging for the chiefs from the various wilps, he did not know how many representatives had received Blue Cloud's message, and their response to it. He would summon his staff to prepare food for chiefs from all the wilps, with the hope that the upcoming event would be peaceful.

Remaining daylight hours were spent by Blue Cloud telling his patrol members his plan and their roles in it. Arriving chiefs and their assistants were to seek shelter in the nearby forest, and remain hidden until the factor had arrived and was seated on the outdoor designated bench. At a hand signal, all were to come forward, surrounding the factor with rifles ready to fire on command. Any attempt by the factor to leave was to be forcibly repulsed.

Mid-morning the following day resembled an annual potlatch. Canoe after canoe arrived from up and downstream of the Skeena River. Many of the chiefs and their assistants walked through the forest trails from their permanent wilps. Agent Blackstone and his assistants had prepared meals of canned meat, potatoes, berries, and rice from the government supplies. The food, combined with the meeting of old friends, provided a festive atmosphere until Blue Cloud interrupted the celebration with directions on how the clansmen were to behave in the presence of the factor. All were to remain hidden until signaled to rush forward in their warrior's apparel and surround the seated factor.

By midafternoon, all had eaten, hidden, and watched for the approaching train from Prince Rupert. Four passenger cars came to a halt at the depot. The conductor opened the door, lowered the steps, and made way for the factor and five assistants, all dressed in their black business suits. Agent Blackstone greeted the visitors and directed them to benches on the depot lawn. Blue Cloud appeared in his combat gear and told Agent Blackstone to tell the visitors that Blackstone would interpret the conversation for both parties.

Fig. 9 Factor and associates meeting with
Agent Blackstone and Blue Cloud

When the visitors were seated, Blue Cloud, standing on a shorter bench, raised his arm. The surrounding woods suddenly came alive with images of ninety screaming clansmen, who encircled the seated visitors. Surprised and frightened by the unusual scene, Factor McKenzie ran for the station platform. He tried to escape through the line, now three abreast, when two of the clansmen grabbed his arms and vigorously threw him to the ground. As he lay moaning, they picked him up, feet dragging, and seated him roughly on the bench.

When quiet was restored, Blue Cloud spoke in a loud Gitxsan tongue to the waiting warriors. Agent Blackstone relayed the message to the visitors.

"He said if anyone else tries to run, shoot them all, and we'll deal with the next group sent here by the government."

Agent Blackstone's announcement had an immediate effect on the visitors. Factor McKenzie was seen waving his arms as he talked to his assistants, presumably telling them to sit still and listen to Blue Cloud's demands.

Interpreting Blue Cloud's words, Agent Blackstone said, "You will all stay here tonight. We will serve supper, after which you will be locked in the depot storage room for the night. One at a time will be allowed to use the latrine. Doors will be locked until daybreak tomorrow. After breakfast, five assistants will board the train, along with Agent Blackstone. Factor McKenzie will remain here until all the Gitxsan children at the residential school have arrived safely at Hazelton two days from now. Tomorrow morning, Factor McKenzie will send another message to Director McLeod, demanding the children's release, with instructions about their transportation to Prince Rupert and Hazelton. Any delay in bringing the children home, you," pointing at Factor McKenzie, "will disappear in the traditional Gitxsan way, and no one will ever see or hear from you again. My patrol will stay here tonight to make sure that you are safe."

Blue Cloud's speech was interrupted by Agent Blackstone, who had just received a telegram. He read the message, then spoke with

Blue Cloud, who indicated that the telegram be read to the factor and his assistants. Agent Blackstone read:

"Factor McKenzie: Avoid confrontation with Indians. Stop. Expect immediate compliance. Stop. Commissioner McNeil. Stop. CC Director McLeod, Agent Blackstone."

Stunned expressions appeared on the faces of Prince Rupert's contingent. Commissioner McNeil's telegraph was a direct order, in opposition to the factor's plan to quell the anticipated Gitxsan uprising by continued negotiations. Blue Cloud's plan could now be executed as he had articulated it. The message to Director McLeod was accepted with delight. Receipt of the telegraph indicated the government in Ottawa was concerned about the effectiveness of the residential school system, in accord with Director McLeod's long-held opinion.

At 8:00 a.m., Director McLeod sent a message, summoning Ms. Crosswhite to his office at 1:00 p.m. At her appearance, he announced that all Gitxsan children were to be sent home, according to governmental orders. Director McLeod knew of the chapel fire at Kamloops. Any attempt at retribution would be vigorously repulsed by the Gitxsan Nation. His orders were to avoid confrontations.

"Tomorrow morning, at 8:00 a.m., I want all the Gitxsan children enrolled at your school to be at the depot, ready to get on the schooner for Hazelton."

"How awful," exclaimed Ms. Crosswhite. "This is terrible news. Where did you get the authority to issue such a message? We were making great progress in changing the ways of these Indian children. Now all they have left is to go back to their heathen ways. What will your order do to the funding from the churches, which is already too low to cover the expenses of educating the Indians?"

"It is not my order. See, it comes directly from Ottawa. This is an indication that your system of taking children from their homes to change their lives is being challenged. The United States has just changed administrators at the Carlisle School, where the system of industrial schools originated. I think Canada will soon do likewise. I advise you to be ready to change the way you have been operating."[5]

Word of the order from Ottawa spread rapidly through the Kamloops School. If the Gitxsan children no longer had to be there, perhaps other children would be able to go home. Happiness consumed the Gitxsan children's lives when they heard the news that they would be leaving. Agoni's passing was still foremost in their minds. They did not know why she died, but they were sure her passing resulted from being at Kamloops. They were ready to go home.

"Time to wake up," announced Teacher June at 5:30 a.m. the next morning. "This is a big day for you. I will miss you, but you will be with your families again. Get dressed, have breakfast, and be ready for the taxi that will take you to the depot."

Children of the Eagle Clan were confused by the rapid change that was being planned for them. Reunion with their families was the best news they had heard since arriving at Kamloops. After breakfast, children were given clothes they had worn upon arrival. The most pleasing part of the dressing process was being able to wear moccasins instead of the narrow, tight leather shoes.

At 7:00 a.m., the departing children climbed onto the taxi for their ride to the depot. Teacher June was there to wave goodbye. Parting, for her, was bittersweet. She had come to love the wonderful children, but she knew that they would be happy returning to their former way of life. She wondered about the long-term effects their stay at Kamloops might have when they assumed a pattern of life that was entirely different from the one they were leaving. Each had been forced to act and think in ways that were different from anything they had ever experienced. How would they adjust to the freedom of everyday living after being subjected to the militaristic régime to which they had been subjected for three months?

---

[5] Officials of Carlisle Industrial School removed Col. Pratt as the leading administrator at Carlisle, in 1900, because his militaristic style of education was deemed ineffective. Carlisle Industrial School officially closed in 1918, at a time when residential schools in Canada were still twelve years from their ascendency.

Nine excited, happy children rode the taxi, bound for the depot, but it left two residents with vastly different emotions about their stay at Kamloops. Ms. Crosswhite, who watched their departure from her office window, saw this as an omen of what the order meant for the entire governmental operation of residential schools. She had built her reputation on the belief that eradication of a culture was most effectively obtained by the complete removal of former associations. Were the tenets upon which she had based her philosophy of education no longer valid? Was this the beginning of her exit as a teacher and administrator? At age forty-five, could she accept and adjust to the changes that appeared on the horizon? She placed her dilemma before her God, as she had done routinely during moments of doubt and confusion.

Teacher June Ames reflected on the events that occurred during her first three months as a professional teacher. She felt confident the principles of education in which she had been immersed at the University of Vancouver were sound and operational. To be effective, they required an environment that permitted opportunities for expression. Currently, there was an indication of mutual rejection for the residential school system, first in Director McLeod's acceptance of her memo, and in the order that Ms. Crosswhite had just received.

Riding the taxi to the depot occurred without the children being aware of its importance. At the depot, they were told to hurry into the schooner, which had waited for their arrival. A two-hour ride and arrival at Prince Rupert were completed without any distractions by the passing scenery or associations with the numerous passengers, who were curious about their recent experiences at Kamloops. Excitement about meeting families whom they had not seen in three months consumed their conversation, now a mixture of Gitxsan and English languages.

Transferring from the schooner to the waiting train involved another reason to hurry through the departure and loading process. Children were told that the next stop, Hazelton, was the place where their parents were waiting. Excitement about the anticipated meeting resulted in children standing, instead of the required sitting, during the ride to Hazelton. Long before the anticipated arrival, children were peering out the windows, in search of familiar faces that would ensure their dreams had become reality.

Arrival at Hazelton was the scene of joy for the children and their parents. Grateful parents greeted their children, without the stoic suppression of emotions. Hugs and kisses were openly expressed, thankful for the removal of their children from a dreadful experience. Agent Blackstone planned arrangements for supper, lodging, and breakfast before their departure the next day. At sunrise, nine canoes containing the emancipated children and their parents made their way upstream on a journey that would find them home by sunset.

Returning the Eagle Clan's children to their homes was viewed as a victory by the Gitxsan Nation. The threat of war by the clans sounded an alarm that drew the attention of governmental officials along the administrative line, ending in Ottawa. Mortification following the outcome of the Riel Rebellion was an ever-present reminder that military force did not solve persistent internal problems. Major changes in present policy regarding the education of Indigenous children were apparent. Leading the crusade for change in policy, surprisingly, came from Factor McKenzie, who saw the present situation as a possibility for corrective action to an impracticable law and, simultaneously, to regain the attention of Commissioner McNeil, an important opportunity he lost with assignment as factor to Prince Rupert.

Using telegraph and written messages via transport by schooner and railroad, he proposed a meeting of six officials most directly implicated by the future threat of their constitution's rebellion. Meetings would be held in Vancouver, including Agent Blackstone, Director McLeod, Blue Cloud, as representative of the Gitxsan Nation, June Ames, as representative of the British Columbia Teachers Association, Professor James Counard, Dean of the College of Education, University of Vancouver, and himself as moderator. Factor McKenzie's proposal received unanimous agreement from suggested participants, who welcomed an opportunity to change a situation which all found ineffective and frequently repulsive.

Meetings of the *Indigenous Children's Education Committee* (ICEC) would be held monthly, with a goal of completion by next

June, prior to implementation of inscription in the fall. Factor McKenzie's suggested list of accomplishments was approved, with an exception that called for amending the ancient Indian Act. As amended, the agenda contained the following actions:

1. Amend the Indian Act, changing "mandatory" to "voluntary" attendance.
2. Curriculum content to devote sufficient time for review of Indigenous customs and their relationship to English ways of life.
3. Qualifications of teachers must include two semesters of education related to words, language, and customs of Indigenous children.
4. Teacher/student ratios should be one to twelve, or less at ages six to ten.
5. Residential schools would be phased out and replaced with day schools. Conscription would end immediately. All displaced children would be permitted to attend their home-based school.
6. Due to frequent hazardous walking conditions, schools would function for six months each year, from May until November.
7. Due to anticipated financial shortfalls, parents of day school attendees would be asked to provide wood for stoves, fish, meat, and fruits for lunches.
8. Government supplies would be distributed to schools as soon as requisitions were received.
9. Teaching of religious content would be forbidden.
10. Day schools would be constructed based on population density.

Discussion of Factor McKenzie's points for action continued with friendly revisions and additions. After five all-day meetings, members agreed their report was ready for submission to Commissioner of Indian Affairs McNeil. Factor McKenzie accepted responsibility for typing and sending the suggested changes to officials in Ottawa, requesting immediate consideration and response.

Delivery of the ICEC report was received with relief throughout the Bureau of Indian Affairs. Commissioner McNeil was pleased to learn that Factor McKenzie had taken the initiative to solve a problem which, if unaddressed, would have become his responsibility. Gaining central governmental approval would require extensive lobbying, but for the present, the threat of rebellion had been quelled. Requests for regional day schools, an increased possibility of being granted considering recent events in British Columbia, would require money and time. Hiring teachers to educate children who do not understand or speak English would be a new challenge, thereby requiring complete revisions of curricula now existing in provincial schools. However difficult, he was convinced the solution would become evident when officials were confronted with evidence that residential schools were an undeniable failure.

Commissioner McNeil was aware of opposition to requests in the ICEC report, delivered by Factor McKenzie. Story Teller Haida's assessment of reaction by officials in Ottawa had been accurate regarding the required action by the Gitxsan Nation, and the governmental response to the nation's potential rebellion. Confrontation directed at their factor, combined with the chapel burning at Kamloops Residential School, initiated a growing concern about education for Indigenous children.

Consideration of Factor McKenzie's report caused Commissioner McNeil to request a meeting with Jean Lefleur, Departmental Secretary of Governmental Finances. After he read the ten requests of the ICEC, including support for schools, teachers, and a special department in Vancouver to oversee the administration of the ICEC, Lefleur exclaimed, "Where do you suggest that we can come up with this kind of support? Your report calls for millions to be sent to British Columbia, a place where we already spend far more than we recover in taxes."

Commissioner McNeil appealed to Lefleur's acknowledged financial ability. "We just avoided an uprising in British Columbia. Military action is much more expensive than education, and only provides a temporary solution. Look at what we lost by fighting the North-West war. Our expenses for educating Indigenous children have been meager, compared to what we spend on White and French children's education."

"I agree with you, but both parties are going to balk at that kind of expenditure. I will present your proposal to the cabinet next week, but first I want Factor McKenzie and Blue Cloud in Ottawa, so they can speak to the cabinet. None of our politicians have ever been west of Winnipeg. They have no idea how vast and rugged British Columbia is, and the children we are trying to educate are considerably more naïve to English customs than those they see daily."

Commissioner McNeil knew that Lefleur's strategy of having Blackstone and Blue Cloud testify would astound the cabinet, especially if they could talk with Blue Cloud, the leader of the suppressed rebellion. McKenzie arranged for Agent Blackstone and Blue Cloud to appear before cabinet members the following Monday. Both natives of British Columbia had been told by McKenzie to appear in their native attire. Blue Cloud, in his customary furs and moccasins, was the center of attention, surprising members with his understanding and command of the English language. Words of wisdom seemed to flow from his lips, spoken in *broken English*, with a Gitxsanion accent. Cabinet members eagerly awaited their opportunity to learn about the governmental history of British Columbia from a sage who had lived through the numerous skirmishes with the Canadian government over land rights and independence.

Intensive questioning of Blackstone, Blue Cloud, and McKenzie continued for two days. Cabinet members were astonished by the daily challenges facing Indigenous people in far-off British Columbia. Their questions involved living arrangements, education, government subsistence, and community life. Agent Blackstone's estimate of the numerous tribes that inhabited northern British Columbia amazed the interrogators. The absence of a census accounted for the mistaken impression that northern British Columbia was devoid of human habitation.

Requirements of the *Indian Act* had always exceeded budgetary provisions by the government. Commissioner McNeil's estimate that only 5 percent of the budget for education in British Columbia was expended for potentially 20 percent of Indigenous children in Canada came as a shocking disclosure. Providing education for thousands, instead of the expected hundreds, of children in British Columbia loomed as an insurmountable challenge. McNeil insisted that the disproportionate spending be addressed in the next budgetary allocation.[6]

Three representatives of British Columbia's Indigenous children left Ottawa convinced that their mission to educate cabinet members had been successful. Aware that their hospitable reception may simply have been a gesture of political protocol, they left convinced that their information was likely to have long-term reverberations. Returning to responsibilities in Hazelton, Prince Rupert, and Vancouver was accompanied by unforeseen expectations. Evidence of their legislative effectiveness appeared in newspapers printed the day they left Ottawa. Appointments for the entire contingent, plus others, had been arranged by Commissioner McNeil and granted by the cabinet.

"Canada to Educate British Columbia Indians" was the headline of the *Ottawa Press*—a resounding declaration in Eastern Canada regarding the cabinet's consideration of the ICEC request. Approval was a direct reaction to the recent unrest among the British Columbia natives. Factor Blackstone's and Blue Cloud's testimony resulted in guilt and political humiliation related to the undeniable neglect imposed on British Columbia's Indigenous children.

Persisting in a favorable atmosphere, Commissioner McNeil proposed the appointment of British Columbia personnel who would initiate the newly approved British Columbia Project, the title applied to the action of the Cabinet. Blue Cloud, because of his ability to negotiate peaceful outcomes, would become Agent of Native Affairs in Hazelton. Agent Blackstone, whose knowledge included all Native tribes in south and central British Columbia, would become

---

[6] First Nations A-Z listing-Province of British Columbia (2017) lists 340 First Nations units, by name, location, region, and tribal affiliation. The number of existing First Nations units in 1900 B.C. was not found.

Factor in Prince Rupert. Factor McKenzie, whose expertise was in Native negotiations, would become Director of Indian Affairs in Vancouver. Director McLeod would become Secretary of the newly created Department of Indian Affairs in Vancouver. Teacher June Ames would become Director of Indian Education, Department of Education, in Vancouver, working closely with Dean Lefleur, College of Education, University of Vancouver. Superintendent Crosswhite, of Kamloops Residential School, given the option to resign or be terminated, chose to return to Ottawa as an administrator in her former position. Kwantum, because of Blue Cloud's insistence, was hired as interpreter and assistant instructor for the Gitxsan children in the newly established school in Hazelton.

Under government supervision, ten day-schools would be established in British Columbia's next fiscal year, ending the mandate of residential school enrollments. Criteria for the schools' location would be determined by population density, indicating that children of the Eagle Clan, because of their remote, northern location, would be required to stay with neighboring clans during the five days of instruction each week. Visitations to homes would be a weekend occurrence, and visitations to the schools by parents would be encouraged.

Honored by their appointments but mindful of their new responsibilities, the administrative contingent resolved to meet monthly in Vancouver. Education of Indigenous children encompassed the responsibilities of all administrators. The effectiveness of their combined efforts would be subjected to annual evaluations. Presently, the confrontational atmosphere that existed between the Gitxsan Nation and the Canadian government had been dissolved by attending to the needs of children.

Summary

Ideas, thoughts, concepts, beliefs, and interpretations associated with the terms *boarding schools*, *residential schools*, and *industrial schools* have a commonality in history, despite anecdotal accounts that they were functioning simultaneously in various parts of the world, namely in South Africa, England, Australia, New Zealand, Scotland, Canada, and the United States. The unifying themes included conscription and custody of children and youth who were orphaned, lived in substandard environments, were neglected or abandoned by their parents, were incarcerated for theft or larceny, and, most frequently, whose standard of living and education were perceived as inadequate or inappropriate for their health and welfare, as assessed by governmental and religious organizations.

History revealed that, despite the universal intention of enhancing the lives of the children who were targeted for conscription and education, these goals were uniformly unattainable because they were routinely overridden by the incessant desire to change the culture of the Indigenous children. Governmental and religious organizations attributed the cause of the children's perceived deplorable living conditions to environmental adaptations that had been developed over centuries of successful survival. The desire to eradicate the children's present culture and replace it with a new lifestyle in a totally different environment proved to be an overwhelming challenge for young children and, financially and administratively, an impossible burden for governmental and religious organizations.

Unceasing attempts to change the Indigenous children's environment, including their religious freedom, is a graphic example of the adage "the end justifies the means." Persons who promoted the concept of "assimilation through deployment" may themselves have been the victims of similar procedures. Many of their ancestors, and currently, the advocates, may have come to America to escape governmental and religious persecution in their native countries. Ironically, the similarity of their previous perceived persecution and the conditions they were advocating for Indigenous children did not seem to be relevant now.

"Manifest Destiny," a doctrine that suggests one race or culture is genetically, and therefore intelligently, superior to another, was a common impression held by many immigrants to the United States and Canada in the nineteenth and twentieth centuries. Concurrently, the idea of group superiority was fortified militarily prior to and during the Indian Wars of the early to mid-1800s. Belief in racial and social superiority was fortified by the rapid western expansion of settlers, who forced the Native Americans into a lifestyle of dependence to which they were unaccustomed. Tribes were compelled to leave their homes and former sources of livelihood. These conditions brought about homelessness, starvation, and thievery—circumstances that were interpreted by governmental and religious organizations as unsuitable ways of living.

Living conditions and tribal customs are described here to erase misconceptions held by governmental officials and those who sought to appropriate the lands now occupied by Native Americans and First Nations tribes. Driven by an identical reason for living, namely, freedom to subsist independently through physical and mental prowess, was the common goal of oppressed and oppressors. Differences of opinion allowed the oppressors, stronger in numbers and resources, to exert their will on those whom they deprived of these essential freedoms.

Governmental officials and religious organizations selected the most vulnerable of all possessions—children of the inhabitants—to attain their goal of assimilation through conscription. Residential schools were selected as the vehicle by which to effectively achieve their reprehensible purpose. Years of turbulence in the residential schools convinced governmental and religious officials that deployment and subjugation were ineffective ways to accomplish assimilation. Mounting evidence caused the closure of many industrial schools in the United States by 1936, substituting day schools to replace the former method of deployment. Despite mounting evidence to the contrary, Canadian residential schools continued to conscript native children in the twentieth century. The last government-supported residential school in Canada closed in 1997.

Kill the Indian, Save the Child: The Residential School Tragedy of Agoni Blue Cloud follows the legislative history of residential schools in Canada from the 1850s to the 1930s to exemplify, despite their contentious existence, similarities between invading pioneers and First Nations tribes. Ethereal needs for independence, freedom to continue desired and traditional lifestyles, and religion of choice were reasons to retreat from oppression by European invaders, but these essentials of human welfare were not endorsed nor extended to First Nations tribes. Extinction of communal support was a devastating burden for the conscripted children but continued as a primary goal for governmental and religious organizations.

The establishment of the *Truth and Reconciliation Commission,* and previous attempts at reparation (see appendix B), recount outstanding efforts by the Canadian government to rectify what was originally believed to be an achievable solution to a perceived problem. Reparation is an appropriate attempt to dissolve the perplexing reality of residential schools, but their shameful existence and dreadful after-effects on the survivors are ever-present.

Sources Relating to Indigenous Residential Schools

The following list of references and sources of information are redundant in the title, but their various sources are included here to inform the reader that abundant information is, and was, available pertaining to unimaginable events that, unfortunately, existed with public knowledge and approval for over one hundred years.

Adams, David Wallace. 1995. *Education for Extinction: American Indians and the Boarding School Experience*, 1874–1928. Lawrence, KS: University of Kansas Press.

Alvarez, Alex. Gary Clayton Anderson. 2015. "Ethnic Cleansing and the Indian: The Crime That Should Haunt America." *The American Historical Review* 120 (2): 605–606.

American Indian Boarding Schools. (Supplementary Curriculum Guide). Mt. Pleasant, MI: Ziibiwing Center of Anishinaabe Culture and Lifeways: 1–7.

Austen, Ian. 2021. "How Thousands of Indigenous Children Vanished in Canada." The *New York Times* (June 7): 1–6.

Barbeau, Manius. 1929. *Totem Poles of the Gitksan, Upper Skeena River*. Ottawa: British Columbia Department of Mines: 1–7.

Barman, Jean. 1996. *The West Beyond the West: A History of British Columbia*. Google Books. University of Toronto Press: 1–255.

Barrera, Jorge. 2018. "The Horrors of St. Anne's." CBC News. https://newsinteractivie.cbc (arch 29): 1–20.

Bear, Carla. 2008. "American Indian Boarding Schools Haunt Many." Morning Ed. NPR (May 12).

Black Hawk. 2008. *Life of Black Hawk, Dictated by Himself.* Penguin Classics.

Brunhouse, Robert L. 1939. "The Founding of the Carlisle Indian School." Pennsylvania History 6 (2): 72–85.

British Columbia First Nations. 2017. "British Columbia First Nations Genealogy." Family Search: 1–5.

British Columbia: Official Centennial Record. 1958. Evergreen Limited Press. Vancouver: 1–179.

British Columbia First Nations. 1998. Glenbow Archives. Calgary, Alberta: 1–5.

Callimachi, Rukmini. 2021. "Lost Lives, Lost Culture: The Forgotten History of Indigenous Boarding Schools." The *New York Times* (July 19).

"Canadian Indian Residential School System." 2024. Wikipedia. https://en.wikipedia.org/wiki/Canadian-Indian-residential-school-system: 1–56.

"Canada's Residential Schools: Missing Children and Unmarked Burials - The Final Report of The Truth and Reconciliation Commission of Canada, Volume 5." 2021. Globe and Mail (June 18).

"Canada's Residential Schools: The History, Part 1 Origins to 1939." 2021. Final Report of the Truth and Reconciliation Commission of Canada. English Web PDF.

"Canada's Residential Schools: The Legacy." 2015. The Final Report of the Truth and Reconciliation Commission of Canada. Vol. 5. McGill-Queen's Press.

"Canadian Residential School System." Wikipedia. https://wikipedia.com/wiki/Canadian_indian_schools.

Carlson, Roy L., and Luke Robert Dalla Bona. 1996. *Early Human Occupation in British Columbia.* University of British Columbia Press.

"Category: Northern Interior of British Columbia." 2024. Wikipedia. https://en.wikipedia.org/wiki/category:Northern-interior-of-British-Columbia: 1–6.

Child, B.J. 1995. *Boarding School Seasons: American Indian Families, 1900–1940.* Lincoln: University of Nebraska Press.

Chisholm, Linda. *Reformatories and Industrial Schools in South Africa: A Study in Class, Colour, and Gender.* University of Witwatersrand. ETD Collection.

"Christianity in Canada." Wikipedia. https://en.wikipedia.org/wiki/christianity-in-Canada: 1–13.

Coletta, Amanda. 2018. "Thousands of Canada's Indigenous Children Died in Church-Related Boarding Schools. Where Are They Buried?" *The Washington Post* (Oct. 21).

Cove, John J. 1982. "The Gitksan Traditional Concept of Land Ownership." *Anthropologica* 84 (1): 3–17.

Curry, Bill. 2009. "Pope Expresses Sorrow for Residential-School Abuses." *The Globe and Mail* (Sept. 19).

Davis, R., and M. Zannis. 1973. *The Genocide Machine.* Black Rose Books. Montreal.

Editors of Time-Life Books. 1973. *The Indians.* Alexandria, VA: 240.

Editors of Time-Life Books. 1994. *People of the Ice and Snow.* Alexandria, VA: 186.

Editors of Time-Life Books. 1998. *Indians of the Western Range.* Alexandria, VA: 184.

"First Nations A-Z Listing." 2017. Province of British Columbia. http://www2.gov.bc.ca/gov/content/environment/natural-re-source-stewardship: 1–9.

"First Nations and Native Americans." 2015. Embassy of the United States, Ottawa, Canada. http://canada.usembassy.gov/visa/information: 1–2.

"First Nations of Canada." Wikipedia. https://en.wikipedia.org/wiki/first_nations_in_Canada: 1–37.

Fournier, S., and E. Crey. 1997. *Stolen from Our Embrace: The Abduction of First Nations Children, and Restoration of Aboriginal Communities.* Douglas & McIntyre Ltd. Vancouver: 1–11.

Fox, Rosemary J. 2006. "Skeena River." *The Canadian Encyclopedia.* https://www.thecanadianencyclopedia.ca/en/article: 2–4.

Fraga, Kaleena. 2022. "Inside the Brutal History of Indigenous Schools in Canada." *The Horrific History of Indigenous Residential Schools in Canada.* https://allthatsintering.com: 1–17.

Fraser, Crystal. 2020. "Resistance and Residential Schools." *The Canadian Encyclopedia*. https://www.thecanadianencyclopedia. ca/en/article. (May 6): 1–18.

Frieson, John. 1997. *Rediscovering the First Nations of Canada*. Detselig Enterprise Ltd.

Gillian, Carol Gear. 1999. "Industrial Schools in England, 1857–1933." https://discovery.uci.ad.uk/id.

"Gitxsan." 2017. *Wikipedia*. https://en.wikipedia.org/wiki/Gitxsan: 1–3.

Glasbrecht, Brian. 2021. "The Misleading Claim that 150,000 Indigenous Children Were Forced to Attend Residential Schools." https://inc/2021/12/19.

Government of Canada. 2115. "Truth and Reconciliation Commission of Canada." Crown-Indigenous Relations and Northern Affairs Canada: 1–9.

Haig-Brown, Celia. 1998. *Resistance and Renewal: Surviving the Indian Residential School*. Vancouver: Arsenal Pulp Press.

Hanson, Eric. 2009. "The Residential School System." *Indigenous Foundations*. arts.ubc.ca: 1–11.

Hauser, Christine, and Isabella Grudlon Pat. 2021. "U.S. to Search Former Native American Schools for Children's Remains." The *New York Times* (June 23): 1–3.

"Hazelton." 2010. http://www.britishcolumbia.com/regions/townID-3: 1–3.

Heidler, David, and Jeanine Heidler. 2023. "Manifest Destiny." *Encyclopedia Britannica* (Dec. 26).

"Homestead Act, 1862." 2009. *History.com*. Editors: 1–5.

Hanson, Erin. 1996. "The Indian Act." *Indigenous Foundations & Arts*: 1–5.

Hopper, Tristan. 2021. "Why so many children died at Indian Residential Schools." *National Post*. May 29. https://history-matters.gmu.edu/d/4929.

"History of Canada." 2010. *Wikipedia*. http://en.wikipedia.org/ wiki/history.

"Historical Background: The Indian Act and the Indian Residential Schools." 2019. https://www.facinghistory.ca/resource-library: 1–6.

"History Matters." 2017. "Kill the Indian, Save the Man. Capt. Richard H. Pratt on the Education of Native Americans." http://historymatters.gmu.edu/d/4929.

"Honouring the Truth, Reconciling for the Future: Summary of the Truth and Reconciliation Commission of Canada." 2015. Truth and Reconciliation Commission of Canada. Web-trc.ca.

Hoxie, Fredrich E., ed. 1996. *Encyclopedia of North American Indians*. Houghton-Mifflin Co. Boston, MA: 739.

"Indigenous People of Canada." *Wikipedia*. https://wikipedia.org/wiki/indigenous_peoples_in_Canada: 1–34.

"Industrial School (Great Britain)." 1999: 1–9.

"In Northern BC. Learn About The Gitxsan." 2018. *Indigenous Tourism British Columbia*: 1–6.

Irujo, Xabier. 2021. "Genocide, Kill the Indian and Save the Man." *Nevada Today* (October 8).

Jacobs, Alan, ed. 1993. *Native American Wisdom*. London: Watkins Press: 186.

Johnson, B. 1988. *Indian School Days*. Key Porter Books. Toronto.

"Kamloops Indian Residential School." 2021. *Wikipedia*. https://wikipedia.org/wiki/Kamloops-Indian-Residential-School: 1–14.

Kelly, Fanny. 2013. *My Captivity*. Skyhorse Publishing. New York, NY: 285.

Kesler, Sam Yellowstone. 2021. "Indian Boarding Schools' Traumatic Legacy, and the Right to Get Native Ancestors Back." *Weekend Edition Saturday*. https://www.npr.org/section/codes.

Little, Becky. 2017. "How Boarding Schools Tried to 'Kill the Indian' Through Assimilation." *History.com*. A&E Television Network (August 17).

Little, Becky. 2018. "Government Boarding Schools Once Separated Native American Children from Families." A&E Television Network (June 19): 1–4.

Lomawaima, K. Tsianina. 1992. "Domesticity in the Federal Indian Schools: The Power of Authority over Mind and Body." *American Ethnologist* 20 (2): 227–240.

Laanela, Mike. 2016. "Orange Shirt Day: How Phyllis Webstad's 1st Day at Residential School Inspired a Movement." *CBC News* (July 7).

Lawrence, Bonita. 2003. "Gender, Race and the Regulation of Native Identity in Canada and the United States: An Overview." *Hypatia* 18:1–3.

Maraniss, David. 2022. *Path Lit by Lightning*. New York: Simon & Schuster Paperback: 837.

MacDonald, David R. 2015. "Canada's History Wars: Indigenous Genocide and Public Memory in the United States, Australia, and Canada." *Journal of Genocide Research* 17 (4): 411–424.

McGreevy, Nora. 2021. "751 Unmarked Graves Discovered Near Former Indigenous School in Canada." *Smithsonian Magazine* (June 28): 1–4.

Mejia, Melissa. "The U.S. History of Native American Boarding Schools." *The Indigenous Foundation*. Retrieved 2-14-24. https://www.indigenousfoundation.org. Date not available: 1–10.

Miller, J.R. 2012. "Residential Schools in Canada." *The Canadian Encyclopedia*. https://www.thecanadianencyclopedia.ca/en/article/residential-schools.

Milloy, John S. 1999. *A National Crime: The Canadian Government and the Residential School System*. Critical Studies in Natural History. Vol. 11, University of Manitoba Press.

Macleod, Rod, Bob Beal, and Richard Foot. "North-West Rebellion." *Canadian History, 1885. Encyclopedia Britannica*: 1–23.

"Manifest Destiny." 2010. *History.com*: 1–6.

Mas, Susana. 2015. "Truth and Reconciliation Offers 94 'Calls for Action'." *CBC News*. https://www.cbc.ca/news.

Merasty, Joseph, and David Carpenter. 2022. "Life Inside a Catholic-Run Residential School for Canadian Indigenous Children." *Time* (September 15). https://time.com/6213238/canada-residential-school-indigenous-children.

Miller, J.R. 1912. "Industrial Schools in Canada." *The Canadian Encyclopedia.* https://www.thecanadianencyclopedia.ca/en.

Mills, P. Dawn. 2008. "For Future Generations: Reconciling Gitxsan and Canadian Law." *The Canadian Encyclopedia.* https://www.thecanadianencyclopedia.ca/en.

Moran, Ry. 2015. "Truth and Reconciliation Commission." *Toronto Star* (August 26).

"Motion to Call Residential Schools Genocide Backed Unanimously." 2022. *The Globe and Mail* (October 28).

"Native American Children." Undated. *Encyclopedia.com.* https://www.encyclopedia.com/children/encyclopedias-almanacs-transcripts-and-maps.

"Native American Daily Life." 2018. *American History.* https://american-history.net/native-american.

"Native American Religion." 2018. *American History.* https://american-history-net/native-american.

"Native American Tribes of British Columbia." 2016. "British Columbia Indian Tribes and Languages." *Canada First Nations.* http://www.native-language.org/british-columbia: 1–5.

Neihardt, J.G. 1988. *Black Elk Speaks.* University of Nebraska Press. Lincoln.

"Native American, First Nation or Aboriginal?" 2017. Drude.com.

Parrott, Zach. 2015. "Government Apology to Former Students of Indian Residential Schools." *The Canadian Encyclopedia.*

Partridge, Cheryle. 2010. "Residential Schools: The Intergenerational Impact of Aboriginal Peoples." *Native Social Work Journal* 7: 33–62.

Pendharkar, Eesha. 2022. "Native American Children Endured Brutal Treatment in U.S. Boarding Schools, Federal Report Shows." *Education Week* (May 11): 1–5.

Pielou, E.C. 1991. *After the Ice Age: The Return of Life to Glacial North America.* University of Chicago Press. Chicago.

Potter, Eleva, and Jerry Jondreau. 2018. "Stories of Place: Ojibwe Knowledge and Environmental Stewardship in the Northwoods." www.susted.com/wordpress/content/stories-of-place-ojibew.

"Population History of the Indigenous Peoples of the Americas." *Wikipedia.* https://en.wikipedia.org/population_history_of_ Indigenous_peoples: 1–21.

Powell, J.V. 2010. "Ts'msyer (Tsimshian)." *The Canadian Encyclopedia.* https://www.thecanadianencyclopedia.ca/en: 1–8.

Powell, J.V., Vickie D. Jensen, and Anne-Marie Pedersen. 2010. "Gitxsan." *The Canadian Encyclopedia.* https://www.thecanadi-anencyclopedia.ca/en: 1–9.

Pratson, Frederich. 1987. *Guide to Western Canada.* 5th ed. The Globe People Press. Old Saybrook Press. Ct: 1–346.

Pratt, B.H. Public domain-no date provided. "The Advantages of Mingling Indians with Whites." *Proceedings of the National Conference of Charities and Correction (U.S.).* Press of Geo. H. Ellis. Boston: 44–59.

"Project of the Heart: Illuminating the Hidden History of Residential Schools in BC." 2015. *The BC Teachers' Federation.*

Ray, Arthur J. 1996. *I Have Lived Here Since the World Began: An Illustrated History of Canada's Native People.* Toronto: Lester Publishing Co.

RCAP. 1996. *Report on the Royal Commission of Aboriginal Peoples.* Volume 1: Looking Forward, Looking Back. Ontario, CA: 310.

Reich, Susana. 2008. *Painting the Wild Frontier: The Art and Adventures of George Catlin.* Clarion Books.

Reimer, Gwen. 2010. "The Indian Residential Schools Settlement Agreement's Common Experience Payment and Healing: A Qualitative Study Exploring Impact on Recipients." Aboriginal Healing Foundation.

"Residential School Locations." Truth and Reconciliation Commission of Canada (TBC). www.trc/ca/about-us/residential-schools-html.

Rice, Kylie. "Residential Schools and Their Lasting Impact." *The Indigenous Foundation.* Retrieved 1/17/2024. https://www. theindigenousfoundation: 1–6.

Rice, B. 2005. *Seeing the World with Aboriginal Eyes.* Aboriginal Issues Press. Winnipeg.

Rivera, Eileen. 2010. "Canadian Homestead Act." *Ehow.* http:// www.ehow.com/about_6080084: 1–3.

Schultz, J.H. 2010. *My Life as an Indian*. Skyhorse Publications. New York, NY: 425.

Seefeldt, Vern. 2011. *Lost in the Canadian Wilderness: What Happened to Louie Harris?* Xlibris. Indianapolis: 191.

Seefeldt, Vern. 2017. *Survival in the Canadian Wilderness: The Legend of Louis Harris*. Dorrance Publishing Co., Pittsburgh: 170.

Siggins, Maggie. 1994. *Riel: A Life of Revolution*. Toronto: Harper Collins: 1–150.

"Skeena River." 2010. *Answers.com*. http://www.answers.com/topic/skeena-river: 1–12.

"Skeena River." 2017. *Wikipedia*. https://en.wikipedia.org/wiki/Skeena-River: 1–4.

Skjervan, Kelly. 2021. "751 Unmarked Graves Found at Former Saskatchewan Residential School." *Global News* (June 24).

Smith, Joanna. 2016. "Truth and Reconciliation Commission's Report Details Deaths of 3,201 Children in Residential Schools." *Toronto Star* (August 26).

"Truth and Reconciliation Reports." 2023. https://ca/records/reports/: 1–6.

"Stage Three: Displacement and Assimilation." 2003. *Government of Canada Web Archive*.

Stanley, George F.G. 1973. *The Birth of Western Canada: A History of the Riel Rebellions*. University of Toronto Press. Toronto, Canada: 474.

Stanley, Steven. 2008. "Louis Riel." *The Canadian Encyclopedia*.

Sterritt, Neil. 2020. *Mapping My Way Home: A Gitxsan History*. Smithers, BC: Creekstone Press.

Taylor, Colin F. 2002. *The American Indian*. Running Press.

"10 Facts About Residential Schools." 2017. https://www.10_facts_about_residential_schools.

Todd, Thornton, and Collins. 2001. "Terminology of First Nations, Native, Aboriginal and Metis." *Web Archive*. https://web.archive.

"The Residential School System." 2009. *Indigenous Foundation: University of British Columbia*: 1–9.

"Timeline Indian Residential Schools." 2115. *Indigenous and Northern Affairs Canada* (May 16).

Thompson, Scott. 2018. "Child Rearing Beliefs & Practices in Indian Culture." *Hello Motherhood*. https://www.hellomotherhood.com/article-562289: 1–14.

Titley, Brian E. 1992. *Narrow Vision: Duncan Campbell Scott and the Administration of Affairs in Canada*. Vancouver: University of British Columbia Press.

Thompson, Scott: 201.

Treuer, David. 2012. *Rez Life: An Indian's Journey Through Reservation Life*. Grove Press. New York, NY: 330.

Vola, James M., and Dorothy Denneen. 2007. *Family Life in Native America*. Greenwood Publishing Group.

Waxman, Olivia. 2022. "The History of Native American Boarding Schools is Even More Complicated than a New Report Reveals." *Time* (May 12).

White, Jon Manchip. 2003. *Everyday Life of the North American Indian*. Dover Publications. Mineola, NY: 256.

Woolford, Andrew. 2015. "This Benevolent Experiment: Indigenous Boarding Schools, Genocide, and Redress in Canada and the United States." *Journal of American History* 103 (2): 487.

Yu, Jane. 2009. "Kill the Indian, Save the Man." *Dickinson College Archives*. https://pabook.libraries.psu.edu/literary: 1–4.

Appendix A

Titles and Terms Used to Describe the Compulsory Education of Conscripted Indigenous Children

Titles and terms used to describe the compulsory education of conscripted Indigenous children in Canada and the United States vary, reflecting the confusion and turmoil associated with the identification of conscripted individuals and their education after deployment:

- *Aboriginal Residential Schools*
- *Aboriginal Schools*
- *American Indian Boarding Schools*
- *American Indian Missionary Schools*
- *Canadian Indian Residential Schools*
- *Federal Boarding Schools*
- *Government Industrial Schools*
- *Indian Industrial Training Schools*
- *Indian Residential and Boarding Schools*
- *Indian Residential Schools*
- *Indian Schools*
- *Indian Training Schools*
- *Indigenous Boarding Schools*
- *Industrial Schools for Indians*

- *Industrial Schools for Indians and Half-breeds*
- *Native American Schools*
- *Native Residential Schools*
- *Nineteenth-Century Indian Boarding Schools*
- *Residential School Systems*
- *Residential Schools*
- *Tallahassee Manual Labor School*

Appendix B

A Chronology of Laws, Acts, Regulations, and Amendments that Governed the Operation for Residential and Industrial Schools for Indigenous Children in Canada and the United States

(The following chronology combines the history of residential and industrial schools in the United States and Canada because their attempted methods of assimilation occurred in parallel during the years of forced conscription.)

Appendix B is not a complete list of references and their sources, both of which were too numerous and often redundant, making it impossible for the author to identify the initial source of information. Appendix B is included to inform readers of the comprehensive chronology and scope of official laws and legal documents associated with the regulation of residential schools in Canada and the United States.

- **1600**—The worldview held by Europeans, based on the *Discovery Doctrine*, was that colonizers were bringing civilization to savage people who could never civilize themselves.

- **1694**—*Fr. White, of the English Province of the Society of Jesus,* established a mission in what is now Maryland. The chief of the resident Indian tribe was told the mission's purpose was to extend civilization and instruction to his ignorant people and show them the way to heaven. (This is an example of how the concept of "Manifest Destiny" was already present in the minds of early missionaries and settlers.)

- **1769**—The *local community of Hanover, New Hampshire,* established a school for native children. This school eventually became Dartmouth College, which has retained some of its programs for Native Americans to this day.

- **1776**—The *U.S. Continental Congress* authorized Indian Agents to employ ministers as teachers for the instruction of Native American students.

- **1778–1871**—The U.S. *government* initiated 389 treaties with American Indians. Most of the treaties involved sales of the Natives' land in exchange for material goods or land intended for use as reservations.

- **1789**—In a *letter from Henry Knox to George Washington,* he suggested that it would be impracticable to civilize the Indians of North America.

- **1816**—A Protestant-supported *Foreign Mission School opened in Cornwall, Connecticut,* for a variety of non-Christian, male students. Most enrollees were from foreign countries.

- **1819**—The *U.S. Congress* appropriated $10,000 to hire teachers and maintain its residential schools.

- **1834**—*Brantford, Ontario,* was the first residential school in Canada. Administered by the Anglican Church, it was also the longest-functioning residential school, closing in 1970. Over the course of its one-hundred-year existence, over 150,000 Indigenous children were placed in residential schools nationally.

- **1831–1996**—Over three hundred residential schools operated in *Canada.* During the 165-year history of

Canadian compulsory education for Indigenous children, an estimated 150,000 children participated in residential school programs.

- **1845**—The *Canadian Bagot Report*, officially *The Report of the Affairs of the Indians in Canada*, was seen as the official document for the operation of the federal residential school system.

- **1847**—On May 26, Egerton Ryerson wrote to the *Canadian Superintendent of Indian Affairs*, "The North American Indian cannot be civilized or preserved in a state of civilization (including habits of industry and sobriety) except in connection with, if not by the influence of, not only religious instruction and sentiment but of religious feelings."

- **1857**—The *Canadian Gradual Assimilation Act* and the *Gradual Enfranchisement Act* were established prior to the Federation. These acts assumed the inherent superiority of the French and British ways. These acts awarded sixty acres of land to any Indigenous male who could demonstrate sufficient advancement in the elementary branches of education.

- **1862**—On May 20, President Lincoln signed the *United States Homestead Act*, which allowed any male who could show six months of residency to purchase land from the government for $1.25 an acre. To make a claim, residents paid $18 for a filing fee, which provided a six-month temporary claim on the land. The *Homestead Act was repealed in 1976*, after 270 million acres had been claimed (10 percent of land in the United States) and 1.6 million claims had been filed in thirty states.

- **1867**—The provinces of *Canada* undergo Confederation.

- **1867**—Passage of the *British North American Act* required the Canadian government to provide education for Indigenous children.

- **1867**—The provision of the *Indian Peace Commission*, by an Act of the U.S. Congress, stipulated the English language was to be used to educate Native children.
- **1869**—President Ulysses Grant ordered that only one religious order at a time, per reservation, could support schools for Native children. This order was given to eliminate the competition between religious orders for enrollment of Indigenous children in specified settings.
- **1871**—The *U.S. government* prohibited further treaties with Indian nations and also passed an *Appropriations Act* requiring the establishment of *day schools* on reservations.
- **1873**—The U.S. *Board of Indian Commissioners*, in a report to Congress, argued that day schools were ineffective because they allowed Native children to spend too much time in their homes, contrary to the policy of assimilation.
- **1875**—*Lt. Richard Pratt*, assigned to supervise seventy-two Native prisoners of war in St. Augustine, Florida, introduced the concept of European-American culture (*immersion and assimilation*). Based on his success, he used this model to develop the Carlisle Indian Industrial School, which then became the template for all government schools in the U.S. In 1879, more than 300 schools in the United States, following this model, had opened.
- **1876**—Passage of the *Indian Act*, an act that consolidated all previous legislation pertaining to Indigenous children, required the *Canadian government* to provide education for Indigenous children. The Canadian government adopted the residential-industrial educational model of the United States—a partnership between the government and various church organizations. This act made attendance at day schools, industrial schools, or residential schools mandatory for Indigenous children.
- **1879**—*Report on industrial schools for Indians and Halfbreeds* (known as the *Davin Report*), which advocated a partnership between government and churches. This also marked the opening of the first off-reservation Native

American boarding school in *Carlisle, Pennsylvania*. Today it is the site of the U.S. Army War College. During the four decades of its operation, an estimated eight thousand students attended the Carlisle school, and nearly two hundred of them are buried in the school's cemetery. The Davin Report advocated that the best way to assimilate Indigenous people was to start with children in residential settings, away from their parents.

- **1880**—Passage of the *U.S. Education Policy* relied heavily on religious organizations to administer and conduct education in the industrial schools.

- **1883**—The *Canadian Parliament* approved $43,000 for three industrial schools—Battleford was the first of federally funded industrial schools.

- **1887**—The U.S. *Congress passed the Compulsory Indian Education Act*, which made it mandatory for Native American children aged six to sixteen to attend federally funded schools.

- **1891**—The *U.S. Compulsory Indian Education Act* allowed federal officers to forcibly remove Native children from their homes and reservations and enroll them in residential schools.

- **1891**—The *Canadian government* reduced the already meager salaries of administrators and staff, stopped funding operating costs, and established an annual per-student allocation of funds. This fund was systematically reduced until, in 1937, the *annual* allocation was $180 per student, which led to an increase in recruitment and a desire to make the schools self-supporting by using the students as forced laborers. This per capita regulation drastically reduced the quality of education, thereby forcing qualified staff members and teachers to seek other means of employment.

- **1890**—*Kamloops Residential School,* formerly named *Kamloops Industrial School,* was established. In 1892, the Canadian government charged the Oblates of Mary Immaculate with control of the school. Kamloops

Residential School attained its peak enrollment of five hundred conscripted children. The school closed in 1978.

- **1894**—Amendments to the *Indian Act* made school attendance mandatory for Canadian Indigenous children.

- **1900**—U.S. *government subsidies* were paid to Native American families for work the Native children were performing in non-native homes. In 1900, there were 1,800 students participating in this "outing system."

- **1902**—*The U.S. Bureau of Indian Affairs* authorized twenty-five off-reservation, federally funded schools to operate in states and territories, with a total enrollment of over six thousand students. Most of the residential schools were established on reservations, where they were commonly administered by religious organizations. At the peak of federally funded schools for Indigenous children, the Bureau of Indian Affairs was supporting *350 schools*.

- **1918**—*The U.S. Carlisle Boarding School* was closed because Pratt's method of assimilation through off-reservation schools was deemed ineffective for the education of Native children.

- **1928**—*The U.S. government's Department of Interior* commissioned the *Brookings Institution* to conduct a survey (*known as the Meriam Report*) assessing the overall conditions of the American Indians in relation to the government's programs and policies. The report recommended the abolishment of the uniform course of study, which taught only European-American cultural values. It also suggested that Native children should be taught in community schools close to their homes and that the *Bureau of Indian Affairs* should provide education and skills that Native children need to adjust to their own and to United States society. The report also noted that infectious diseases were often widespread in the boarding schools due to malnutrition, overcrowding, unsanitary conditions, and overwork.

- **1930**—The *Canadian government* realized that the residential schools were unsustainable and that they were failing to meet the desired objective of assimilating Indigenous children.

- **1931**—The number of *Canadian residential schools* operating at one time *peaked at eighty.*

- **1936**—Robert Hoey, superintendent of *U.S. Welfare and Training in the Indian Affairs Branch*, opposed the expansion and opening of additional residential schools. In their place, he proposed the opening of day schools located near the children's reservations. This proposal was resisted by the United Church, the Anglican Church, and the Catholic Church, which insisted that greater intensification of present methods was the correct answer to assimilation.

- **1945–1955**—During this ten-year period, the number of First Nations children enrolled in day schools conducted by the *Canadian Indian Affairs Branch* grew from *9,533 to 17,947.*

- **1951**—An amendment to the *Canadian Indian Act* allowed federal officials to establish agreements with provincial, territorial, and school boards regarding the education of Indigenous children in public schools. Despite the shift in policy (Section 88 of the Indian Act), the removal of Indigenous children from their homes continued through the 1970s.

- **1953**—The *U.S. Congress* passed *Concurrent Resolution 108*, which stated that the government should, as rapidly as possible, end the policies making Native Americans wards of the government, thereby granting them all the rights of full citizenship.

- **1968**—*U.S. President Johnson* ended the practices of *Concurrent Resolution* and directed the Secretary of the Interior to establish Indian School Boards in federal Indian schools.

- **1969**—*The U.S. Bureau of Indian Affairs* operated 226 schools in seventeen states.

- **1969**—*The Canadian residential school system* was transferred to the *Department of Indian Affairs*, ending the involvement of religious organizations in the education of Indigenous children.

- **1972**—The *U.S. Congress* passed the *Indian Education Act*, which advocated a comprehensive approach to meeting the needs of American Indians, thereby recognizing that American Indian and Alaskan Native children have unique educational and cultural needs. This *act* also encouraged the relocation of Indian people away from reservations toward urban locations, thus reducing the enrollment of Native children in boarding schools and instead placing children in public schools.

- **1975**—*The U.S. Congress* passed the *Indian Self-Determination and Education Assistance Act*, which guaranteed tribes the right to determine their own futures and the education of their children.

- **1983**—*The Canadian Department of Indian and Northern Affairs*, in a report entitled *Native Children and the Child Welfare System*, written by Patrick Johnson, estimated that between 1960 and 1990 an estimated 11,132 children throughout Canada and the United States were taken from their homes without the consent of their parents.

- **1996**—The *final report of the Royal Commission on Aboriginal Peoples* was released, recommending a public investigation into the violence and abuses at residential schools, and brought the experiences of former students to public attention.

- **1997**—The last *Canadian* publicly funded residential school, Kivalliq Hall in Rankin Inlet, *closed.*

- **2005**—*Enactment of the Residential Schools Settlement Agreement*, in which the *Canadian government* allocated $1.9 billion in compensation for survivors of abuse in the residential schools.

- **1998**—The *Canadian government* announced the publication of *Gathering Strength, Canada's Aboriginal Action*

Plan, including the establishment of the *Aboriginal Healing Foundation and a Statement of Reconciliation.*

- **2001**—*Indian Residential Schools Resolution Canada* was created as a separate department with the mandate to address the legacy of Indian residential schools.

- **2005**—The Canadian government launched an *Advance Payment* program for eligible former Indian Residential School students who were sixty-five or older.

- **2006**—The *Indian Residential School Settlement Agreement* was approved by all parties to the agreement. It was the largest class action settlement in Canadian history.

- **2007**—The *Canadian Indian Residential Schools Settlement Agreement* resulted from demands from former students of residential schools for recognition and restitution and a formal apology. An estimated *150,000 First Nations and Métis children* attended the residential schools, and an *estimated six thousand children died* while enrolled in the schools.

- **2008**—On June 1, the *Canadian Truth and Reconciliation Commission* was established. Its purpose was to uncover the truth about the residential schools.

- **2008**—Canadian *Prime Minister Harper*, on behalf of the government, offered an apology to all former students of the residential schools.

- **2010**—The *Truth and Reconciliation Commission* held its first national event in Winnipeg, Manitoba.

- **2014**—The *Truth and Reconciliation Commission* held its final event in Edmonton, Alberta.

- **2015**—Publication of the *Truth and Reconciliation Commission Report*, outlining the areas in which the *Canadian government* failed in its goals and standards for residential schools. Estimates suggest that *3,200 Indigenous children died* in the residential schools. The report contained *ninety-four "calls to action,"* urging all levels of government to work and advance reconciliation.

- **2021**—*The Canadian government* established September 30 of each year as the *National Day of Truth and Reconciliation.*

- **2021**—Summary of the *final report* of the *Truth and Reconciliation Commission* estimated at least *3,201 children died* while enrolled in the residential schools, with the possibility the number may exceed six thousand.
- **2021**—In May, the remains believed to be those of 221 children were found buried on the site of the *Kamloops Indian Residential School,* identified by using ground-penetrating radar.
- **2021**—In June, an estimated 751 unmarked graves were found on the site of Marieval Indian Residential School in *Marieval, Saskatchewan.*
- **2021**—In June, the Lower Kootenay Band reported the discovery of 182 unmarked graves near the Kootenay Indian Residential School in *Cranbrook, British Columbia.*
- **2022**—The *Canadian Government House of Commons* unanimously passed a motion recognizing the residential school system as genocide.
- **2022**—On April 1, *Pope Francis* apologized for the conduct of some members of the Roman Catholic Church for their roles in the *Canadian residential school system.*
- **2023**—The *National Native American Boarding School Healing Coalition* released the names of *523 Indian boarding schools* known to have operated in *the United States.*

Appendix C

Excerpts from the Final Report
of the Truth and Reconciliation
Commission (TRC)

An abbreviated account of the *final report of the Truth and Reconciliation Commission* is included here as an indication that oppression and denial of freedom are consistent problems to be obliterated by incessant surveillance. Enumeration of the areas where changes in policies and actions were requested by Indigenous Peoples of Canada reminds us of our heritage and the struggle for freedom endured by our ancestors.

(All reports issued or created by the *Truth and Reconciliation Commission* are in the public domain. Digital copies may be accessed or duplicated at no charge. Full print copies of the TRC reports can be purchased from McGill-Queen's University Press.)

The Canadian Indian Residential Schools system (IRS) acquired its legacy with the passage of the *Indian Act in 1876,* mandating the Canadian government to provide education for Indigenous children. Prior to the Indian Act, the government, in 1845, received *The Report of the Affairs of the Indians of Canada* (unofficially called the Bagot Report), which was interpreted as the official document for the establishment of the Federal Residential Schools System.

In 1884, attendance at IRS schools became mandatory for Indigenous children. Conscription of native children continued thereafter, reaching its summit in 1930, with church-supported funding, eighty residential schools were operating in Canada, at a time when industrial schools in the United States were being phased out.

Numerous lawsuits against the Canadian government, alleging abusive treatment of enrollees, eventually led to the 2007 *Indian Residential Schools Settlement Agreement* (IRSSA)—a class-action resolution against the Canadian government that included five components:

1. The Common Experience Payment
2. Independent Assessment Process
3. The Truth and Reconciliation Commission
4. Commemoration
5. Health and Healing Services

Establishment of the Truth and Reconciliation Commission was accompanied by seven goals:

1. Acknowledge residential schools' experiences, impacts, and consequences.
2. Provide a holistic, culturally appropriate, and safe setting for former students, their families, and communities as they come forward to the Commission.
3. Witness, support, promote, and facilitate Truth and Reconciliation events at both national and community levels.
4. Provide awareness and public education to Canadians about the IRS system and its impacts.
5. Identify sources and create as complete a historical record as possible of the IRS system and its legacy.
6. Produce and submit to the parties of the Agreement a report including recommendations to the Government of Canada concerning the IRS system and experience, including the history, purpose, operation, and supervision of the IRS system; effects and consequences of IRS (including systemic

harms, intergenerational consequences, and impact on human dignity); and ongoing legacy.

7. Support the commemoration of former Indian residential school students and their families in accordance with the Commemoration Policy Directive.

Summary of the Conclusions Reached by the IRS in Its Final Report

- Survivors of the IRS system were subjected to malnutrition; physical, mental, emotional, spiritual, and sexual abuse; unsafe living conditions, including exposure to extreme temperature, mold and mildew, and overcrowded sleeping quarters; extremely high rates of infectious diseases; and more.

- At least three thousand two hundred children died while in the custody of the IRS system, though Justice Murray Sinclair, TRC chair, estimates the death rate is as much as ten times higher due to poor record-keeping.

- Indigenous youth are extremely overrepresented in the child welfare system.

- Despite making up just more than 5 percent of the total population, Indigenous Canadians account for more than 30 percent of the prison population in Canada.

- Indigenous Canadians have significantly reduced life expectancies and suffer disproportionately from diabetes, hypertension, substance abuse, mental health concerns, and overall morbidity and mortality as a direct result of social determinants and trauma, according to the 2019 analysis published in the *Journal of Health Equity*.

- A 2017 meta-analysis of sixty-one studies supports these assertions. The effects of the residential schools on Indigenous Canadians are intergenerational and multifaceted, negatively impacting mental and physical health.

- Access to safe housing and other essential services and items (such as clean drinking water) is severely limited.

- The mistreatment of Indigenous Peoples from the early days of colonization is directly responsible for the negative stereotypes and stigmas associated with Indigenous Canadians today.
- Moreover, the IRS system (along with other anti-Indigenous government policies) had a direct impact on current policies that make it more difficult for Indigenous People to access funding, healthcare, education, and other resources that would build equity in their communities.

Taken together, the reality of residential schools and their legacy is disturbing, and Indigenous Peoples are still suffering the consequences of colonization.

Based on the Conclusions Listed Above the IRS issued "94 Calls for Action"

The *94 Calls to Action (CTAs)* are recommended policies meant to aid the healing process in two ways: acknowledging the full, horrifying history of the residential school system, and creating systems to prevent these abuses from reoccurring. The CTAs are in two categories: *Legacy* (calls 1 to 42) and *Reconciliation* (calls 43 to 94). The calls, by category, subcategory, and numbers within the subcategory, are listed below:

Legacy

- Child welfare (calls 1 to 5)
- Education (calls 6 to 12)
- Language and culture (calls 13 to 17)
- Health (calls 18 to 24)
- Justice (calls 25 to 42)

Reconciliation

- Canadian Government, UN Declaration on the Rights of Indigenous Peoples (calls 43 to 44)
- Royal Proclamation and Covenant of Reconciliation (calls 45 to 47)
- Settlement Agreement Parties and the United Nations (calls 48 to 49)
- Equality for Aboriginal People in the Legal System (calls 50 to 52)
- National Council for Reconciliation (calls 53 to 56)
- Professional Development and Training for Public Servants (call 57)
- Church Apologies and Reconciliation (calls 58 to 61)
- Education and Reconciliation (calls 62 to 70)
- Missing Children and Burial Information (calls 71 to 76)
- National Centre for Truth and Reconciliation (calls 77 to 78)
- Commemoration (calls 79 to 83)
- Media and Reconciliation (calls 84 to 86)
- Sports and Reconciliation (calls 87 to 91)
- Business and Reconciliation (call 92)
- Newcomers to Canada (calls 93 to 94)

About the Author

Vernal (Vern) Seefeldt (1933-) is a distinguished professor emeritus at Michigan State University, East Lansing, Michigan. His life began in a three-room farmhouse in Grover Township, northern Wisconsin. Immersed in the culture of a German community, he enrolled in a one-room elementary school, unable to speak English. Enrollees in the country school ranged from twenty-one to thirty-six, taught by one teacher, whose advanced education culminated with a two-year certificate, issued by a county normal school.

His attendance at Lena High School resulted in a salutatorian award and ten varsity athletic letters. Vern attended La Crosse State College (now the University of Wisconsin-La Crosse) on an academic scholarship, graduating with majors in biological science and physical education. His initial teaching job terminated with induction into the U.S. Army deployed to the Historical Division, Karlsruhe, Germany, where the mission involved interpreting World War II combat strategies from captured German documents. While deployed there, he established a working relationship with Oberst General Franz Halder, Hitler's deposed and imprisoned Chief of Staff, incarcerated for his opposition to Germany's simultaneous engagements on western and eastern fronts.

Karlsruhe became the off-post home of Nancy, a teacher of art whom he met while both taught in Oconomowoc, Wisconsin. They were married on September 5, 1957, in a mandatory civil ceremony, and two days later in a religious ceremony. Deployment ended with an honorable discharge and return to Madison, Wisconsin, where Vern began graduate study at the University of Wisconsin, Madison, graduating in 1966 with a PhD and cognates in anatomy and human movement science.

His tenure-track employment began at Michigan State University (MSU) in 1966 and closed there with his retirement, at age sixty-two, in 1995. Vern's specialties in child development and youth sports led to lectureships in eight foreign countries, always accompanied by Nancy, a connoisseur of museums and art galleries. He received numerous honors, culminating with the Hetherington Award, issued by the National Academy of Kinesiology in 1998.

In addition to Nancy, the Seefeldt family includes daughter Lynne, son-in-law Jesse, son John, daughter-in-law Karen, granddaughter Kayla, and grandson Ross.